ZARA PHILLIPS

Other Books by the Author

ZARA PHILLIPS

A Revealing Portrait of a Royal World Champion

Brian Hoey

For my children and grandchildren

First published in Great Britain in 2007 by
Virgin Books Ltd
Thames Wharf Studios
Rainville Road
London
W6 9HA

A catalogue record for this book is available from the
British Library.

ISBN 978 1 905264 04 9

The paper used in this book is a natural, recyclable product
made from wood grown in sustainable forests. The
manufacturing process conforms to the regulations of the
country of origin.

Typeset by TW Typesetting, Plymouth, Devon
Printed and bound in Great Britain by
Mackays of Chatham PLC

CONTENTS

INTRODUCTION

Young, attractive, a World Champion. Along with her first cousin, Prince William, Zara Phillips has become the acceptable face of modern Royalty in the twenty-first century. In William's case, his boyish good looks, undoubted charm and self-deprecating sense of humour (and the fact that he will one day be King) have all captured the public's attention; in Zara's, it is her unconventional lifestyle, amiable easy-going spirit and devil-may-care attitude that have made her one of the most popular Royals. Banished for good are the former stuffy images of the Royal Family as figureheads and remote characters who could scarcely be approached – and certainly not touched by mere mortals. The age of deference and reverence that characterised the early days of the reign of Elizabeth II, when Royalty was spoken of in hushed tones and men and women practically genuflected at the mere mention of their names, has disappeared forever.

Today, William and Zara's generation of the Royal Family generate an impression that is a formidable combination of star quality and the common touch. Zara has become a role model for young women, with her feisty, outgoing personality, glamorous rugby international boyfriend and her own world title-winning sports achievements. Zara has beauty, independence, sporting success and style. And of course it helps that Zara is very photogenic, in fact a photographer's dream, as picture editors throughout Britain and abroad will testify. The tabloids love to show her in one of her latest outfits, riding gear, or even better, kissing her boyfriend in an off-guarded moment. In person she is even better looking, with a lightly tanned, golden-brown complexion, gleaming white teeth, soft, blonde, shining hair, flashing pale greeny blue eyes and a steady, focussed gaze. Her face lights up when she smiles and while she exudes a sense of robust and healthy well-being, combined with a girl-next-door kind of whole-someness, she possesses a figure full of erotic promise, or, as one of her fellow equestrians put it, 'She has a backside that makes walking behind her – especially when she's going upstairs wearing tight jodhpurs – one of life's greatest pleasures.'

Zara is arguably the most natural woman in the Royal Family, with a friendly laugh and an accent that is difficult to place. It's not cut glass or aristocratic, like her grandmother, the Queen, but neither is it completely estuary English. It's more lower middle class than anything else, a result of her education at the local village school, followed by Gordon-stoun and university. She is also the most tactile of Royals since the late Diana, Princess of Wales. When Zara is talking to someone, she occasionally will lean forward and touch them on the arm to emphasise a point. Her mother, the Princess Royal, would never do that. Nor would any other member of the Royal Family, with the possible exception of Zara's cousin, Prince Harry, who is another 'toucher and hugger'.

Zara was just six weeks old when I first set eyes on her. She was sleeping peacefully in her pram – it was one of those beautiful Silver Cross models that you could get in any colour you liked, as long as it was black, and had been the favoured transport for upper- and middle-class infants for many years. The iconic British product had been the favourite pram for generations of Royal babies and it has now become the required baby carriage for rock stars' children and Hollywood parents. Zara was lying in the conservatory at Gatcombe Park, the home of her mother and father, Princess Anne (as she was known then – the Queen bestowed the title Princess Royal, which is only ever given to the eldest daughter of the sovereign, on Anne in 1987) and Mark Phillips. I had been working with the Princess for some months on her biography – little knowing that twenty-four years later it would be her daughter who would be my subject. Princess Anne had worked until just four weeks before the birth, and some six weeks after Zara was born I was invited to Gatcombe to start again. When we had finished our session for the day, the Princess rather shyly asked me if I would like to see the new baby. I've always liked babies, having fathered three of my own, so I said I would be delighted. I had already, four years earlier, seen Anne and Mark's first child, their son Peter, just after he was born, and at that time there was little indication of any particular maternal feelings on the part of the Princess. This time though, as she leaned into the pram to show me Zara, there was no doubt that she was besotted.

I have to admit I barely glanced at the baby before making the appropriate noises about how beautiful she was, and leaving.

Since then, I have observed Zara on many occasions, and read about her exploits as she rose through the ranks of national and international equestrianism. I have also followed her thoroughly modern lifestyle in the media, along with thousands of others. She is an unusual member of the Royal Family, and in spite of the fact that her mother went to great pains when she and Peter were born to stress – rather ingenuously – that they are not Royal, '. . . their Grandmother just happens to be Queen,' both children are as much part of the Royal Family as their first cousins, Princes William and Harry and Princesses Beatrice and Eugenie. Princess Anne went against her mother's wishes when she refused to allow her children to be granted titles – Peter was the first grandchild of a sovereign to be born without a title in five hundred years. Anne felt, and she has yet to be proved wrong, that a title would hinder them as they tried to make their own way in life as they grew up. They cannot deny their Royal lineage, and neither of them would wish to, but it has been slightly easier for them to live what passes in Royal terms for a normal life without the millstone of an anachronistic title hanging round their necks.

The 'no-nonsense' attitude of the Princess Royal has been very influential in the upbringing of both her children, and she has always welcomed the fact that they do not have, what she terms, the 'disadvantage' of being called Prince or Princess. But there is a problem. While the Princess Royal might like to believe that Zara – and Peter – are not Royal, no one else is ever likely to allow them to forget for one moment that their grandmother is Queen and that they are in direct line of descent from Queen Victoria. But if it is a millstone Zara is going to be burdened with for the rest of her life, she shows little outward sign of being weighed down by it. And neither does she deny that doors have opened to her because of who her mother and grandparents are. She is also well aware that some people try to cultivate her, without success, in the hope of ingratiating themselves with the Royal Family. Zara treats it all like a big joke.

Her thoroughly modern lifestyle: having already lived with two boyfriends, first with the National Hunt jockey Richard Johnson, with whom she enjoyed – if that is the right word – a turbulent, on and off relationship for three years before dumping him, and more recently with the Gloucester and England rugby player Mike Tindall, with whom she currently shares a home in a cottage on her mother's estate at Gatcombe Park, has marked her out as a young woman who makes her own rules.

In between she has hit the headlines many times at home and abroad, particularly when she appeared at the late Queen Mother's 100th birthday party showing that she had had her tongue pierced and was sporting a metal stud, plus a diamond in her navel. Surely Zara is the only member of the Royal Family to flaunt tradition in such an open manner and reveal her rebellious nature. And her outfits have attracted considerable attention and comment, not always for the best reasons.

Zara has an enviable figure, and several of her dresses have shown a little more of it than perhaps the Queen might have wished. As one fashion expert remarked, 'With a bosom like hers and the way she shows it, you can certainly tell she's not a boy.'

But when the situation demands, Zara can be as conventional as any other member of the Royal Family. Attending Royal ceremonies such as the funerals of her great-grandmother, Queen Elizabeth the Queen Mother, and her great aunt, Princess Margaret, whom she admired greatly, and who she resembles in her attitude to life, Zara was the picture of decorum, dressed in traditional black and, apart from her striking blonde hair, which has benefited from the occasional highlighting, looking indistinguishable from any of her Royal relations. She may be the most outgoing member of her family, but the Windsor streak of rigid self-discipline runs right through her. In other words, she knows the form.

Zara's sporting achievements speak for themselves. She was European and World Champion at the time she was 25 in a sport where, as her mother once told me, 'the horse is just about the only thing on the course who doesn't know you are Royal.' Zara has dedicated herself to becoming the best in a field that receives comparatively little publicity and where the competition is among the fiercest in the world. Her best year to date was 2006, with victory in the World Championships as well as being voted BBC Sports Personality of the Year, winning a third of the thousands of public votes cast. She knew she was in the running for the BBC award, but when she and her boyfriend turned up at the NEC in Birmingham for the ceremony, which was televised live, she genuinely had no idea that she had won. Her surprise when the announcement came was absolutely real, as was made clear when she received the trophy and made what to many of the millions watching on television was one of the most excruciating acceptance speeches ever. Later, one of her mother's Ladies-in-Waiting confirmed that Zara had not prepared a speech simply because she really didn't believe she was going to need one. Her public relations advisers must have been squirming with embarrassment, as they had not prepared her for the eventuality of winning either. So much for professional, highly paid spin-doctors.

The icing on the cake came at the end of 2006 when Zara and Mike were invited to Buckingham Palace to attend the Achievers of the Year reception. As the Queen moved along the line, meeting her guests and chatting politely, she came upon her granddaughter and instead of the usual handshake, there was a loving kiss bestowed, and they talked for several minutes before Her Majesty moved on. Zara wasn't there as a family member but as a genuine 'achiever' in the equestrian world, and her skill was recognised two weeks later when it was announced that she had been awarded the MBE in the New Year Honours list. She had been told some weeks earlier, but, like all recipients, she had been sworn to secrecy until the official announcement in the London Gazette. It was a fitting finale to a spectacular year. And this wasn't 'Granny Windsor' showing favour to her granddaughter; if that had been the case, the honour would have been membership of the Royal Victorian Order, the Sovereign's personal order of chivalry. The award of an MBE (Member of the British Empire) comes on the 'advice' of the Prime Minister through the Honours Committee at Number 10 Downing Street, although, as the Fount of All Honours, the Sovereign has to give her final approval.

The interviews conducted after her World Championship win revealed more about Zara than just her riding preferences. It turns out Zara has incredibly simple tastes – she really is just a regular girl (or woman – she is, after all, in her mid-twenties). She was asked what other career she might have chosen if she had not taken up riding and said, 'Maybe fashion or interior design.' Zara said her favourite colour is blue and she prefers to wear jeans above all else. If anyone wants to cook her a meal, pasta should be on the menu and she said – probably with tongue in cheek – that Lucozade orange is her favourite drink. On films she mentioned *Gladiator* and *Lord of the Rings*, with Nicole Kidman as her choice for best actress, but admitted that she doesn't really read when asked to nominate her favourite book. She loves music, with Robbie Williams and Counting Crows high on her list of all-time greats and, not too surprisingly, she said that Aston Martin – the preferred motor of her uncle, Prince Charles – is her favourite car, though what her sponsors, Land Rover, would make of that would be interesting to hear. Finally, she admitted that Australia and New Zealand are her favourite places in the entire world, 'because it is incredible there and because of the people.' The answers Zara gave revealed an insight into her personal preferences, which were not all that different from many other young women of her age and class. If the same questions were asked in, say, two years time, no doubt the answers would be very different.

Zara's love life has kept the tabloid newspapers enthralled in recent years, particularly when she moved into Richard Johnson's North Cotswold home and then sold an exclusive interview and twelve pages of photographs to *Hello!* magazine. The reaction of Princess Anne – and the Queen – has not been revealed, but neither would dream of criticising Zara publicly, no matter what their private views might be. Princess Anne doesn't really care about media reaction anyway; she got so used to being the Royal they all loved to hate when she was younger that she feels her family may as well do whatever they want, because the press will report whatever they like anyway.

Zara's relationship with her current live-in boyfriend, Mike Tindall, who was part of the World Cup-winning England rugby side in 2004, has ensured frequent appearances in the gossip columns, where they are described as one of the country's most glamorous young couples. They don't court publicity, but neither do they go out of their way to avoid it, as they regularly appear at charity functions where they know they are going to be photographed. If they happen to have a drink in their hands, or are being openly affectionate, so much the better for the press.

No one who knows Zara was in the least bit surprised that she chose a man with no title and little money as a lover. After all, her mother's first husband was hardly the choice most people would have thought suitable for the only daughter of the Sovereign. He did not come from an aristocratic back-ground (his father was sales director for Walls sausages), and there was no great family fortune or large country estate, but Mark was an accomplished horseman, arguably better than Anne herself. And Princess Anne's second husband, Tim Laurence, Zara's stepfather, was considered even less qualified, as he had been a servant of the Queen for three years, as naval equerry, before marrying the Princess in a move that horrified senior courtiers. But the Royal Family, knowing that Anne was a woman who made her own decisions, accepted both Mark and Tim, even if, at first, they were more than a little surprised and reserved. Friends of Zara and Mike say the secret of their success is that her Royal relations do not overawe him, and the fact that his own sporting accomplishments speak for them-selves. Mike Tindall was already successful on the rugby field before he met Zara, in the same way that Mark Phillips was a better rider than Princess Anne when they first met – and that was what attracted her to him in the first place.

Those who know Zara well say there was no way she would have linked up with anyone who was not a successful sportsman, which explains her relationships with both John-son and Tindall. She may have attended university, but by no stretch of the imagination could she be described as an intellectual. She loves the company of sportsmen and women and she plainly enjoys the celebrity her own success has brought her.

Zara's circle of friends include both Royal and non-Royal young men and women. She is particularly close to her cousin Prince William, who is just one year younger, and he says, tongue in cheek, that she has no respect for his rank, often reducing him to helpless bouts of giggling at the most inopportune moments. He was once reported to have jokingly reprimanded her saying, 'Don't you know you are speaking to your future King?'

With parents like hers (Princess Anne was European three day event champion in 1971 and Mark Phillips won a team gold medal at the Olympic Games in the same sport), it was perhaps inevitable that Zara would follow in their footsteps, even if her brother, Peter, prefers his horsepower to be under the bonnet of a Formula One racing car. Her mother said she never tried to force Zara into the saddle, but admits her daughter was only two years old when she rode her first pony, so it was hardly her own choice, at least initially.

As she grew up Zara developed into a keen and enthusiastic sportswoman, hunting alongside her parents in Gloucestershire (before it became illegal) and even playing hockey for Cheltenham Ladies College for a season. She also loves horse racing, but at the time of writing, she has yet to emulate her mother's success as a jockey on the Flat, though she has ridden in a couple of races for charity. One of Richard Johnson's pals said if she ever did take it up, there'd be a hell of a queue in the showers afterwards.

Along with her brother, Peter, Zara is the beneficiary of a substantial trust fund set up by the Queen when she was born, one of the trustees being her Godfather, Andrew Parker Bowles. Brigadier Parker Bowles, an early boyfriend of Princess Anne, has remained on the best of terms with the Royal family in spite of his divorce from Camilla, now the Duchess of Cornwall, and as an ultra-competitive rider himself – he twice took part in, and completed, the Grand National at Aintree – he supports Zara at every opportunity.

Like her mother, Zara doesn't suffer fools gladly, and while she accepts, with good-natured, resigned tolerance, the intrusion of the media as part of the price she must pay for her success, she rarely gives interviews and then only about her equestrian involvement. A paid interview with *Hello!* magazine was a one-off that is yet to be repeated. She learned at an early age to deflect questions about her Royal relations without appearing to avoid the issue or give offence. Most reporters who meet her come away with the impression that here is a down to earth, no-nonsense young lady who has achieved success on her own merits, not because of her connections. She works hard and plays hard and when she appears in the early hours of the morning at a nightclub or fashionable restaurant on the arm of her live-in companion, few realise that she has probably been up since five thirty mucking out and preparing her horse for a day's training. Some people imagine that because she is a member of the Royal Family all she has to do is turn up and ride the horse in competition, leaving all the dirty work to someone else. Nothing could be further from the truth. Zara works as hard as anyone in the stables and her team know that with her there is only one standard: perfection. She may be a hard taskmaster but she pushes herself harder than any of them.

When she became World Champion in Aachen, Germany, in 2006, she was the first to acknowledge that the success was entirely a team effort, not hers alone. But the people who work with and support her say that while it may be a team, there is no doubt who is the captain of the team. She is prepared to listen to advice – especially from her parents – but she does not always follow it. Mark Phillips says if she had, she might have been even more successful at an earlier age than now. Though it's hard to see how becoming World Champion at 25 could be bettered.

Those who work with Zara say she has the Royal way of making everything sound like a reasonable request when you know that she is really giving an order, and that she expects to be obeyed instantly. Patience is not one of her virtues.

Because Zara's mother refused to allow her to have a title when she was born, she has been able to grow up with a measure of independence previously unknown in the Royal Family. She likes to refer to herself as a 'semi-detached' member of the most famous family in the world. But when she marries, Royalty will occupy the first rows of pews in the church with at least two future Kings of England in the congregation. And if and when Zara has children of her own, their grandmother will be a Princess and their great-grand-mother a Queen. Their great-uncles and great-aunts will be princes and princess, with the occasional duchess thrown in for good measure.

This then is the story of an extraordinary young woman, a 'non-Royal' Royal, who has found herself propelled into the limelight – and who, at the moment, appears to be thoroughly enjoying the experience.

1 SPORTS PERSONALITY OF THE YEAR

'And the winner is ... Zara Phillips.' To judge by the stunned reaction of Zara, and most of the audience, the result came as a complete surprise. The competition was to find the BBC Sports Personality of the Year for 2006, and while Zara knew she was on the short list of nominees, she, like the 'experts' in such things, had expected Ryder Cup golfer Darren Clarke to win.

The year 2006 was a vintage one for Zara Phillips. As well as being crowned Three Day Eventing World Champion in Aachen, Germany, in August, it had been just twelve months since she had won the European eventing gold medal, becoming only the third rider to win both championships, World and European, in a single year.

Zara had every reason to feel pleased with herself. Two years earlier she had not even been considered among the leading riders in Britain, never mind the world. Now she had reached the pinnacle of her sport, number one in the world, and she was being recognised by her peers, something that gave her the greatest satisfaction of all.

Previously she had been known only as the daughter of the Princess Royal and, more often, as the granddaughter of the Queen. It was a description that rankled with her even more than the 'Royal rebel' tag that she had worn for years, as she wanted, above all else, to be acknowledged as someone in her own right, for her own achievements, not just for her Royal connections.

When she was chosen for the first time to represent Great Britain at the World Equestrian Games in Germany in August 2006, it was because she was the best rider available, and when she won the world title, it was a complete vindication of the selectors' decision. So Zara had every right to feel more than satisfied with what she had achieved in such a short space of time, and in one of the toughest of all sports.

The fact that the Queen and the Duke of Edinburgh, no mean equestrians themselves, so obviously shared her delight made 2006 such a particularly special year and one she will remember the rest of her life. Now Zara was following in her mother's footsteps by winning the BBC Sports Personality of the Year award to crown a magnificent year. Princess Anne had won the award 35 years before in 1971 and Zara's victory marked the first time two members of the same family had won. It was also only the third time an equestrian had won; Olympic show-jumper David Broome was the first, in 1960.

Zara's dad, Mark Phillips, had nominated his daughter for the award and was determined to be present at the ceremony, so he cut short one of his many trips to the United States, where he coaches the national Olympic three day event team, and flew home just in time to join the studio audience.

Zara received almost a third of the 680,000 votes cast by phone and text and when she received the prestigious trophy, she paid an emotional tribute by dedicating it to the memory of her friend Sherelle Duke, who had been killed in a tragic riding accident just before the final of the World Championships. Zara had also dedicated her victory in Aachen to Sherelle, saying 'I went out and got my gold medal for Sherelle. I dedicate everything I win to her and to all the people who help and support me.' Unlike some other sports celebrities, Zara is a firm believer in collective recognition. The BBC awards, which were broadcast live on television from the National Exhibition Centre in Birmingham, will be remembered not only for the fact that Zara won, but also for her acceptance speech. Proving that she genuinely had not expected to win, Zara had not prepared even the briefest of notes – and it showed.

Watched by her boyfriend, father and stepmother (her mother did not attend, saying it was Zara's night and she did not want to take any of the attention from her), Zara made one of the most painfully inadequate speeches of all time, rivalling in awfulness the worst and most embarrassing acceptances made at that pinnacle of show business 'Luvviedom' – the Oscars. Some claimed that the word 'amazing' was used no fewer than 30 times in two minutes; some of those in the audience reckoned it was more like 50 times. Perhaps it just sounded like it.

'I'm actually shaking,' she said. 'This is amazing. It's amazing to be here with all these fantastic people. I'm sat in awe of everyone. And to win this is absolutely amazing.' Luckily she wasn't too amazed to thank all the people who had voted for her.

The Princess Royal could, and perhaps should, have given her a few pointers before the show, as she is never at a loss for words. But, presumably, as Zara employs a professional public relations company with expert speech writers, the Princess didn't think she would be needed. While Zara has inherited many of the undoubted equestrian skills of her father, she obviously also possesses his 'talent' for off-the-cuff public speaking.

The show was watched on television by the Queen at Windsor Castle and she was thrilled as her granddaughter's name was announced as the winner. So too were the parents of Zara's boyfriend, Mike Tindall, as they watched at home in Yorkshire. For Mike, it was a particular pleasure as he had been part of the England World Cup-winning squad that had won the team award three years earlier.

Princess Anne was interviewed for the programme about Zara's progress as a horsewoman. She commented, 'She is a natural – always was. From her earliest time on a pony, she was always in the right place.' When she was asked how it felt not to be actively involved but watching from the sidelines instead, she replied, 'It is a slightly mixed blessing . . . On the basis of having done it, you would like to be more involved, but you just have to stand back and be around and be there for them.'

Interviewed by the BBC afterwards, Zara told the audience that the Queen had taken a keen interest in her activities. 'She has had horses all her life, so she knows what goes into the sport and how hard I have worked,' Zara said.

Later Zara said she hated award ceremonies, even though it was fantastic to be recognised, and great for her sport. She added, 'It's not my favourite thing to do . . . I don't like having to stand there. I hadn't prepared myself to win, that's why I was so shocked when we [her horse Toytown and her] won. It was a nice shock.' It was also the moment when Zara's dislike of the spotlight had to be thrust into the background. Even winning the World Championship had meant little exposure outside the equestrian world, but this award, in front of thousands in the studio audience and millions watching on television, meant she would no longer be allowed to be a private person; from then on, she was public property.

Before the awards were announced, Zara sat enthralled as 23 sporting legends were invited on to the stage to rapturous applause from the 3,000-strong audience. Former heavy-weight champion Sir Henry Cooper, who had presented Princess Anne with her award in 1971 – and who had retired long before Zara was even born – was there, as were the former snooker World Champion, Steve Davis, Olympic gold medal triple jumper, Jonathan Edwards, Open golf winner, Nick Faldo and rugby union star, Jonny Wilkinson, whose last-minute drop goal in Australia won the World Cup for England. Zara couldn't believe she was in the same company as these heroes and that shortly her name would be engraved alongside theirs on the trophy.

It wasn't only Zara who was thrilled to see these legendary figures. As a team player, Mike is a big fan of those sportsmen and women who reach the top through their own efforts, without having the support of a squad. He said later that he admired Tiger Woods and that in individual sports there is a lot more pressure on that person: whether they win or not, it's just down to them.

Most years, the result of the BBC award is a foregone conclusion. There may be one or two names that emerge as likely winners, but when Faldo, Cooper and Olympic oarsman Sir Steve Redgrave were the winners, they were clear favourites for months ahead and no one was surprised when their names were read out. In 2006 the list of possibles wasn't anywhere as grand as previous years, and with few outstanding performances to attract the public's attention, it could have been anybody's day. Three day events, golf and gymnastics (gymnast Beth Tweedle was third) are not especially high-profile sports, except perhaps when a golfer wins a major tournament, so the field was acknowledged to be among the weakest in the 52-year history of the award. But that should not detract from Zara's achievement; she thoroughly deserved to win and to receive the plaudits of the crowd. It's just that in an Olympic year, if a three day eventer and a 100-metre sprinter both win gold medals, you can be sure which one will be Sports Personality of the Year – and it won't be the one who rides a horse.

Nevertheless, by winning the title, Zara focussed the spotlight on her sport in a way that would have cost thousands if she had had to pay for the publicity. She also gave herself an even higher profile than she had enjoyed since becoming World Champion four months before. And she knows how important it is for her to remain in the public eye if she wants to keep the sponsors who pay her vast sums of money to promote their products. They are happy only when they see her, and whatever they want her to advertise, in the media. As many other celebrities have discovered to their cost, being out of the limelight for too long can also mean being out of pocket.

The award was warmly welcomed by other equestrians throughout the world. The President of the Federation Equestrienne Internationale, Princess Haya Bint Al Hussein, declared, 'Zara's achievements in Aachen this summer were remarkable in any circumstances. I was then and remain now, highly impressed not only by her obvious sporting ability, but also by her competitive spirit. We are thrilled to have such an exceptional personality as an ambassador for our sport.'

However, Zara's victory also resulted in snide remarks from a certain section of the media. The respected *Daily Mail* sports correspondent Alan Fraser wrote that it was a bad year (for the competition) in which 'a bit of posh with blue blood' won over the rest. The presenter of the BBC programme, Gary Lineker, in an attempt at humour, described Zara as 'posh tottie' – apparently he intended it to be a compliment – while elsewhere her win was slated as a success for privilege and style over substance in a lean year for British sport. But at the party that followed the awards show, praise was heaped on Zara from all sides. The other winners from previous years were generous in their comments, even though most of them had never heard of three day events, or if they had, only in the context of Zara's mum and her famous 'naff off' comments to reporters in the days when she was competing.

As the night went on, the champagne flowed freely, but Zara didn't really need it; she was already drunk on success and the heady atmosphere of the occasion. It was a wonderful evening and a fitting climax to a spectacular year. She later said it was one of the best nights of her life – even if she did not like award ceremonies.

Writing a newspaper column after the ceremony, commentator Lucinda Green said, 'What she has achieved is extraordinary. But what is even more remarkable is that she won the World Championships on the back of an intervening year from hell with the younger horses she is educating. Her season – and her body – were peppered with unspectacular moments when her horses fell or refused . . . But she soldiered on, her friends . . . and her own strength of character keeping her afloat . . . She has guts as well as class.'

Just a few months after the BBC awards, Zara received another accolade: she was awarded an MBE in recognition of her contribution and achievements in her sport. Her Majesty was tickled pink to present Zara with the honour at an investiture ceremony in the State Ballroom at Buckingham Palace, and was heard to murmur that it was the 'icing on the cake'. It was a fitting end to an incredible year.

The British team manager, Yogi Breisner, says Zara's recent success has brought more public interest in the sport than ever before and that she is a brilliant person to have around as her presence takes a lot of pressure off the rest of the team.

With the European and World titles, plus other awards such as Sports Personality of the Year and the MBE, Zara has been acknowledged as one of the outstanding riders of her generation. When it came to competing at the highest level in one of the most dangerous sports on earth, she showed that she can ride like a champion and win like a champion. With skill and determination, a formidable combination in itself, she also possesses a total belief in herself and her ability to take on all comers. She has displayed the courage that is required when faced with conditions that would force lesser riders to flinch. That's the difference between the great and the merely good.

2 EARLY DAYS

On Wednesday, 5 November 1980, it was announced from Buckingham Palace that Princess Anne was expecting her second child, to be born in May 1981.

The news was released at that moment only because Anne and Mark Phillips had just told the Queen, at a belated 50th birthday party for Princess Margaret at the Ritz Hotel in London, and they knew that it would not be possible to keep it a secret after the guests found out. The last to be told were the paternal grandparents, Peter and Anne Phillips, who were not invited to the party. The expectant parents had been unable to tell the Phillipses the news because the future grandparents were not at home in Wiltshire, but were staying in a remote part of Cornwall, at a holiday cottage that did not have a telephone. Princess Anne was determined that her mother- and father-in-law, with whom she had always got on very well, would not find out from newspapers or on the radio, so she contacted the local police, or at least, had one of her protection officers do so, to ask them to send someone to the Phillipses' cottage asking Anne Phillips to telephone her 'urgently'. When Mrs Phillips received the message she was very concerned, not knowing what it was all about. Her call to the Princess eventually came from a public phone box, and the Princess told her, 'Thank goodness I reached you. I'm pregnant.' Both sets of grandparents were overjoyed at the news.

The Queen's oldest granddaughter was born at 8.15 in the evening on Friday, 15 May 1981, just a couple of months before the young lady who was to become the most famous woman in the world, Lady Diana Spencer, married into the Royal Family, becoming Princess of Wales and, as everyone thought at the time, the future Queen. At the time of her birth, Zara was sixth in line to the throne, the highest any non-titled female had ever been. She is now eleventh, following the births of Prince William, Prince Harry, Princess Beatrice and Princess Eugenie, the daughters of Prince Andrew, Duke of York, and Louise, the daughter of the Earl and Countess of Wessex.

Zara should have been born on the 8th, but chose to arrive a week late. Her mother had wanted to give birth at home, but had been convinced that a hospital was a safer, more appropriate choice. Anne had been determined that she would not go into hospital for the birth and she told the Queen that if she couldn't have the baby at home in Gloucestershire, then at least Windsor Castle would be preferable, as it was nearer to London should an emergency arise. But Her Majesty supported the Royal gynaecologist, George Pinker, who had delivered the Princess's first child, Peter, four years earlier, when he insisted that the private Lindo Wing of St Mary's Hospital in Paddington was the best place. It was in the same suite, at the same hospital, that the Princess of Wales would later have both her sons, William and Harry.

Three other doctors assisted Mr Pinker: Sir Richard Baylis, the Queen's Physician, Mr Clive Roberts, Consultant Gynae-cologist, and Mr David Harvey, Anaesthetist. It was a normal birth, with no complications, so in fact baby Zara could have been delivered at home, as the Princess wanted.

Zara weighed in at a healthy 8 pounds, 1 ounce and her father was a reluctant witness to the birth. He declared later that it was certainly an experience he would not wish to repeat, adding, 'Yes, I was present at the birth, but I wouldn't recommend it to other fathers.'

The Queen saw her granddaughter for the first time when she visited the hospital on the evening following the birth, and Prince Andrew, Anne's favourite brother, arrived shortly afterwards carrying a large bouquet of carnations.

Mother and child both recovered well and they remained in St Mary's for only three days before returning to Gatcombe on Monday, 18 May. It was to be three weeks before Anne and Mark revealed the name they had decided on for their daughter. Princess Anne surprised everyone, including the Queen and Prince Philip, by choosing a name that was unusual to say the least for a member of the Royal Family. No one seemed to have heard the name Zara before, apart from Prince Charles, who actually suggested it. I asked the Princess how the choice came about. 'The baby made a rather sudden and positive arrival and my brother thought that Zara [a Greek biblical name meaning "Bright as the dawn"] was appropriate.' The name also means 'Princess' in Greek and Arabic. I later spoke to both parents about the name and each one said they had never heard it before. Yet one of the Princess Royal's most long-serving and senior Ladies-in-Waiting, the Hon. Shan Legge-Bourke (whose daughter, Tiggy, became very well known as the nanny of Princes William and Harry, and was later at the centre of an embarrassing row with their mother over allegations that she had had an affair with their father) also had a daughter whose name was Zara, so it was practically impossible and highly unlikely that the Princess, at least, had not heard the name mentioned before.

Princess Anne has always presented a regal and, at times, unfeeling public face – so much so that people who do not know her sometimes think she is a hard woman without the normal maternal instincts one expects of a mother. Nothing could be further from the truth. She may be expert at hiding her emotions and controlling any outward display, but the birth of Zara showed just how emotional she could be. She was besotted with her new baby. Shortly after Peter was born, the Princess attempted to play down the so-called joys of pregnancy, remarking that it was an occupational hazard of being married, and 'something of a bore. Being pregnant is a very boring nine months.' She added, 'I am not particularly maternal.' Zara changed all that.

I happened to be at Gatcombe working with Her Royal Highness on a television documentary and book at the time of Zara's birth. We had suspended operations shortly before the baby was expected and some six weeks later, I was invited to see the Princess to discuss when we could start again. The birth of Zara did not prevent Princess Anne from carrying out 84 Royal engagements during the year her baby was born, or a further 168 the following year.

After our short meeting, the Princess asked rather shyly if my producer and I would like to see Zara, who was sleeping in the conservatory attached to the house. During the months we had been working together, we had established a relationship that could best be described as friendly without being familiar, and correct rather than cordial. I had grown used to the fact that she did not enjoy small talk and that when she was 'on duty' she was single-minded to a degree that meant she ignored everything and everyone – including her personal police bodyguard and Lady-in-Waiting . . . and me – in order to concentrate on the job in hand. But when she showed us Zara for the first time, there was no doubting the maternal pride and love that shone in her eyes. It was revealing, comforting and rather endearing to find that the woman we had all thought of as a hard-bitten Princess could be just as soft-hearted as the rest of us. She was obviously getting an enormous amount of pleasure from this tiny bundle of joy who had just entered the world.

The Princess Royal may have wanted to have her baby at home, but when it came to the christening, there was never any doubt that it would be a traditional Royal ceremony, held in the oldest occupied castle in Europe. The service took place in the Private Chapel at Windsor Castle at 11.45 a.m. on Monday, 27 July 1981, with Zara Anne (after her mother, of course) Elizabeth (after her grandmother) being held over the Royal font by the Dean of Windsor, the Rt Rev Michael Mann, one of Prince Philip's closest friends and a former fellow officer of Mark Phillips in 1st The Queen's Dragoon Guards. For the christening, Zara wore the robe of Honiton lace that had been worn by every Royal baby since Queen Victoria's children were baptised.

Both the Queen and the Duke of Edinburgh were present, as were Mark's parents, Major and Mrs Peter Phillips, and Princess Anne had chosen the Godparents herself. They were a mixture of friends and family, with the senior Royal being Anne's younger brother, Prince Andrew, who was on leave from the Royal Navy where he was a helicopter pilot (and in spite of his playboy image, Prince Andrew, now the Duke of York, has always taken his duties as Godfather seriously). Among the other Godparents was Helen Stewart, the wife of the former World Champion racing driver Jackie Stewart (Jackie had shared the title of Sports Personality of the Year with Princess Anne in 1971 and he and his wife have remained close friends with the family ever since). Another Godfather was Andrew Parker Bowles who was at that time still married to Camilla (now the Duchess of Cornwall). This was, of course, long before her affair with Prince Charles became public knowledge and brought the name Parker Bowles such notoriety. The Countess of Lichfield, one of Princess Anne's most long-serving Ladies-in-Waiting, and the wife of Society photographer the late Earl of Lichfield, was also a God-mother, and making up the christening party was Hugh Thomas, another old friend and British team mate of Princess Anne's in the equestrian world, who had competed with her in the 1976 Olympic Games in Montreal. Lady Diana Spencer, who was to become very fond of Zara, refused to attend the christening, which took place just two days before her wedding. The official reason was that there was too much to do in preparation for her big day; privately, those close to the Prince of Wales knew that the real reason was that Diana knew Camilla Parker Bowles was invited to attend with her then husband. It was probably the first time that Diana hinted that she knew about Charles's relationship with Camilla, who was also a guest at the Royal wedding in St Paul's Cathedral on 29 July.

Baby Zara behaved with all the serenity of her grand-mother, the Queen, at the christening, unlike her big brother, Peter, who four years earlier had yelled throughout his own christening service. But no one, not even her mother or grandparents, could raise a smile from the infant for the official photographs taken by the Earl of Lichfield. It was the first time the baby had been seen since the birth and her belated appearance inevitably meant that there were rumours that something was wrong with her. The fact was that Princess Anne was determined that her daughter would not be subjected to a barrage of publicity before she, her mother, was ready. The princess had balked at media attention all her life and she saw no reason why she should change her habits just to placate the press. She told me that she had grown used to being very much a 'tail-end Charlie' [to her brother, the Prince of Wales] and that 'You don't think anybody's paying too much attention to you, then you find out that public attention is on you too. It comes as a nasty shock.' She didn't want her children to be brought up in the constant glare of the limelight. That is why she would not allow any photographs of Zara to be taken before the christening. She wanted to postpone the publicity as long as she could. Yet she agreed that both Peter and Zara needed to know, as soon as they were able to understand, that they would be the focus of attention, 'otherwise the shock when it does come is awful.'

A birth in the Royal Family is considered a red-letter day in the national calendar and when Zara arrived on the scene, the newspapers and radio and television stations all ran stories about the baby. Her bloodline was investigated – on both parents' sides. As a direct descendant through the House of Windsor, she was the great-great-great-great-granddaughter of Queen Victoria, who would have been horrified at the thought of any member of her family being born without a title. She would also have forbidden Princess Anne's second marriage to a mere Lieutenant in the army who had no great fortune, estate or aristocratic background to offer. Even as recently as Queen Mary, Zara's great-great-grandmother, who died in 1965, the union would have been frowned upon. When her own daughter, Princess Mary, the Princess Royal, married Viscount Lascelles (later the Earl of Harewood) in 1922, Her Majesty remarked, 'How strange to be marrying a subject.' Princess Anne's grandfather, King George VI, was a stickler for protocol who would often fly into an uncontrollable temper even at such slight breaches of Court etiquette as someone turning up dressed in the wrong outfit. What he would have made of Zara – and Peter – being born without even an 'Honourable' in front of their names can only be guessed at. But Anne and Mark were very relaxed about such matters, although it was reported that on one occasion when a photographer called out to the Princess to 'Look this way, love,' she sharply replied, 'I am not your love, I am Your Royal Highness.' True or not, it made a good story and an even better headline. While Zara's birth did attract a lot of attention (after all, she was then sixth in the line of succession to the throne, in spite of not being a princess), it was not seen as being as newsworthy as the birth of her brother four years earlier.

Peter Phillips arrived on 15 November 1977, just a day after his parents had celebrated their fourth wedding anniversary. He was born at 10.46 in the morning in the Lindo Wing of St Mary's Hospital in Paddington, the first Royal baby in the twentieth century to be born in hospital. Princess Anne had to have the consent of the Queen for the birth to take place outside a castle or palace, and Peter made history by being the first grandchild of a British sovereign to be born a commoner, with no Royal title.

There was enormous interest in Peter's birth, both at home and abroad. Once Mark Phillips had telephoned the Queen at Buckingham Palace to give her the news, the Home Secretary, Merlyn (later Lord) Rees, was the first official to be informed, followed immediately by the leaders of all Commonwealth countries. The Prime Minister, James (later Lord) Callaghan, announced the birth in the House of Commons, while Prince Charles, who was out shooting in Yorkshire was told by short-wave radio, this being long before the days of mobile phones. Prince Andrew and Prince Edward were studying at Gordonstoun in Scotland where they were told they were now uncles. The timing of the announcement also meant that for the first and only time the Queen was delayed for ten minutes in holding an Investiture. She explained her lateness saying, 'I have just had a message from the hospital. My daughter has given birth to a son, and I am now a grandmother.' The audience broke into spontaneous applause – another 'first' at an Investiture. For the Queen, the birth was a double pleasure as 1977 was also the year of her Silver Jubilee.

For the first few weeks of her life, Zara was looked after by Sister Wallace, a trained children's nurse, who wore the traditional uniform of starched apron, collar and cuffs, with the kind of head-dress no longer seen in hospitals or nursing homes. Sister Wallace handled the infant with confidence and assurance, bathing her and changing her nappies before handing her over to her mother, scrubbed and polished, and then putting her to sleep in the cot that had been used by Peter and before him by their mother. By all accounts, Zara was a model baby, and did not give her parents or her nurse any sleepless nights.

Sister Wallace worked under the watchful eye of Mabel Anderson, who had been nanny to Peter for four years and who had announced she was ready to retire a couple of months before Zara was born. She was persuaded to remain for the handover period to her replacement. Mabel Anderson had looked after Royal children for over 30 years and she insisted on the strict discipline of Palace life. She was never seen without a starched uniform and when she had first arrived at Gatcombe, she must have been more than a little surprised at the informality of the house after the homes she was used to. But she adapted brilliantly and coped admirably with the lack of the usual nursery staff she expected.

Once Mabel and Sister Wallace had left, Zara was placed in the capable hands of a no-nonsense Yorkshire nanny, Pat Moss, who came to rule the nursery on the top floor of Gatcombe. Moss, who previously had been Princess Anne's nanny, was a practical woman like the legendary Mabel

Anderson, who is now long retired and still adored by Prince Charles. She was physically not unlike a slimmed-down version of the actress Dawn French, of *Vicar of Dibley* fame, and was well used to the care of upper-class children and young Royalty. But Zara was not allocated a nursery footman, private maid or chauffeur as her mother had been before her. That sort of privilege was restricted to her Royal cousins, William and Harry. Princess Anne was determined that Zara would not get used to a life she would not be able to sustain later on. Not that the child was denied anything she needed. Far from it. She was given the best of everything, from what she ate and drank to the clothes she wore and the toys she later played with.

The difference between Peter and Zara when they were babies was that Peter's day-to-day welfare was left in the hands of his nanny, but when Zara arrived, her mother was decidedly hands-on. Princess Anne was the first Royal mother to actually change her baby's nappies herself and not delegate the task to a servant. She also loved bathing Zara and the chores were shared with Pat Moss when her Royal duties allowed. Once a week Pat had a day off and then it was the Princess who did everything for the children. She would wake them, see that they ate their breakfast, and bathe and dress them. Nobody who knew Anne could believe that she would prefer doing the mundane everyday chores that most mothers take for granted and that her riding was relegated to second place.

As Prince William was just a year younger than Zara and lived at Highgrove, just a couple of miles from Gatcombe, they used to spend many days together during their early childhood. At one time, the area was known as the 'Royal Triangle' because three homes belonging to members of the family were located within a few miles of each other: Gatcombe, Highgrove and Nether Lypiatt Manor, the home of Prince and Princess Michael of Kent until they sold it towards the end of 2006.

William's nanny, Barbara Barnes, and Pat Moss would often meet up at one or other of the houses with the children.

Birthday parties would be held at Highgrove and Gatcombe, and Diana, Princess of Wales, often called on her sister-in-law to chat about their respective offspring. When the four grandchildren of the Queen (the Duke of York's daughters, Beatrice and Eugenie, had not yet been born, and nor had Louise, daughter of the Earl of Wessex) were taken to see the Queen, they were paraded in strict order of precedence with William taking pride of place, followed by his brother Harry, then Peter, with Zara bringing up the rear. None of the children thought there was anything unusual in this; it was the rule and, for them, perfectly normal. Even today, when Zara is invited to Balmoral or Sandringham, she is told the time she has to arrive and she knows that she will have to be there before her Royal cousins, as the more senior relatives are expected to arrive last. The rule applies to everyone in the Royal Family. When all the Queen's children and their uncles and aunts are invited to attend a function such as the Chelsea Flower Show, the Master of the Household issues a printed timetable containing the exact order of arrival, with the junior members being first on the scene and all having to be present when Her Majesty's car arrives. Prince and Princess Michael of Kent would normally be first (and they do not particularly enjoy having to wait for their superiors in the Royal Family to join them). Then comes the Duke of Kent, the Gloucesters, the Princess Royal, accompanied by Tim Laurence, the Earl and Countess of Wessex, the Duke of York, and then the Prince of Wales and the Duchess of Cornwall, who are the last in the cavalcade before the Queen and Prince Philip make an entrance. The route the Royal cars follow has been timed to the minute and traffic is held up all along the way to make sure nothing interferes with the timetable. So it is true that when Royalty is on the move, all traffic lights appear to turn green.

When William and Harry came over to Gatcombe for tea as children, they were dressed as if they were going to see the Queen, with highly polished shoes, white shirts and ties, and trousers with knife-edge creases. By the time they went home, they looked like any other children: scruffy, mud-splattered – and very happy. Princess Diana didn't mind a bit what sort of condition they were in, but Prince Charles, who had never enjoyed a relaxing childhood in casual clothes, disapproved of his children being seen like this. Charles did not often turn up with William and Harry – it was more usual for Diana or the nanny to bring them – but when he did arrive, it caused enormous turmoil in the Gatcombe household. The Prince's car was always preceded by an escort vehicle and followed by two others, all containing armed police. No one else was allowed to be included on the guest list unless His Royal Highness had approved him or her previously, and the menu for lunch or tea was also submitted weeks before the visit. Prince Charles is Peter's Godfather, and has always accepted the role and taken it seriously, but he was never easy with either Peter or Zara when they were children, and was not particularly comfortable with Mark either.

Mark was a natural with his own and other children. He loved William and Harry, and they knew they could get away with practically anything with Uncle Mark. They always wanted to be taken to the stables, much to the dismay of their nanny, who knew she would have to clean them up before they were seen by their parents. But Mark always obliged and if a little muck became stuck to them, he would say, 'So what?'

Prince Charles was a well-meaning man who loved his children as much as any father. The trouble was he simply did not seem to know how to be affectionate in public and became embarrassed if William or Harry tried to hug him. Whereas Mark Phillips would allow either of his children, or his nephews, to climb all over him and wrestle with him on the floor, Charles was far too grand for such informality. A member of the Princess Royal's household said that he was much grander than even the Queen and the Duke of Edinburgh. The Princess has occasionally been impatient with her older brother, but there is a real bond between them and she has been fully supportive of him throughout all his domestic difficulties. One of the Royal policemen said of Prince Charles, 'If only he could unbend a little.'

* * *

With Anne and Mark as parents, it was inevitable that Zara would be introduced to the saddle from an early age. For her Christmas present in 1983, when she was just two and a half years old, she was given a Shetland pony and she was seen the following morning being led around the grounds of Sandringham, where they were spending a holiday with the Queen and Prince Philip. Zara took to riding as naturally as other children take to walking, and within weeks she could trot and canter, with either a Royal groom or one of her parents running at her side. There used to be an old wooden rocking horse in the entrance hall at Gatcombe, and visitors were often intrigued to find Zara sitting on its back, riding it vigorously. She even believed she *was* a horse for a time and her nanny thought she was never going to grow out of it. Princess Anne employed a groom named Debbie in those days, and she was among the first to recognise Zara's potential, saying that the child was going to be a world champion one day. Naturally, no one took her seriously, but it would be interesting to hear what she felt when Zara did eventually win the title.

As Peter and Zara grew older, their mother became stricter. She would not put up with any nonsense from them when they threatened to get out of hand. She didn't mind childish pranks; she has never been obsessively tidy, and when Peter climbed all over the piano in his muddy Wellingtons, she didn't raise the roof. But if either of the children disobeyed her, retribution was fast and furious. One act of disobedience was enough, after that it was a quick smack and off to bed. They soon got the message.

Zara was a very lively child who loved the outdoor life and the staff at Gatcombe soon became used to seeing her and Peter, dressed in dungarees and Wellington boots, climbing trees and playing in the garden. Peter was very much his father's son and Mark was rarely seen on the estate without the youngster in tow, while Zara was obviously her mother's child. One only has to look at photographs of the Princess Royal at the same age to realise who Zara takes after. Physically there is a strong resemblance, and temperamentally they share many of the same characteristics. Even as a young child Zara was determined and knew her own mind – and was not afraid to express her opinions. Observers noted that she had a gleam in her eye and the grown-ups often had a difficult task in keeping up with her. She loved to run and hide whenever she could. Her mother, however, was equally determined that Zara would not be a spoilt child, so her nanny was given a free hand to punish her when she misbehaved.

Peter was always a quieter child than Zara. She was the wild one and would run around frantically, knocking into furniture and occasionally breaking items in the house. Anne was more forgiving towards her than she was to Peter. It wasn't that she cared more for her daughter than her son; she was simply more protective of her.

The Queen and Anne Phillips were doting grandmothers and the children often stayed with one or the other. Her Majesty loved having them with her at Windsor, but she too was of the old school and believed in being firm with small children. She took them on the Royal Yacht every summer, and a naval rating (they were called 'Yotties' on *Britannia*) was always instructed not to let Zara out of his sight. The youngster did her best to hide from him, thinking it was all a great joke, and she sometimes went to extraordinary lengths not to be found. On one occasion the Queen happened to be sitting on deck when Zara came hurtling down the stairs. The Queen realised it was dangerous and that Zara could have seriously hurt herself and told her not to do it. Zara ignored her grandmother and carried on, whereupon 'Granny' grabbed her by the arms and gave her a good shaking. Today that might be called 'child abuse' by the politically correct brigade, but Zara and Granny adored each other. They still do and neither can do any wrong in the other's eyes.

The household at Gatcombe has always been one of the most relaxed of all Royal homes. The butler is often seen wearing corduroy trousers and check shirt in the daytime, and the maids do not wear black dresses and white aprons. But when the occasion demands, formality is the order of the day. A dinner party with the Princess Royal and Tim Laurence invariably means black tie – and on those occasions the butler does dress in full evening wear of tailcoat and white tie. Despite the relative informality of daily life at Gatcombe, Zara was expected to know the form from an early age. She and Peter had their meals in the nursery when they were very young, but as soon as they had learned how to behave with adults, they were included in certain family functions. If the Queen visited, the children were always on display and behaved impeccably with Granny. As Zara grew she also learned the correct way to greet Her Majesty. She would give a deep curtsey, kiss the Queen's hand and – when she was tall enough – bestow another kiss on her grandmother's cheek. Peter did the same thing, with a neck bow replacing the curtsey. It may seem old fashioned these days, but to observe these little examples of perfect manners is somehow rather endearing. It all seems from another age, as indeed her grandparents are, but Royal children grow up learning the form, and curtseying to the Queen is now second nature to Zara, and all the other female Royals. She doesn't even think about it; it just happens.

I once asked the Princess Royal whether she thought of the Queen as her sovereign or as her mother. She told me I had got the question the wrong way round, saying, 'She has been my mother longer than Queen [Anne was born in 1950, the Queen ascended the throne in 1952] so obviously I think of her as my mother first.' Zara feels exactly the same way about both her mother and grandmother. She says she has never really thought about it, as the Princess Royal deliberately kept her and Peter out of the limelight when they were small, so their home life was comparatively normal. And she has only ever known the Queen as her grandmother, so there's no way of her knowing anything different. If there is one thing that is guaranteed to annoy Zara, it is to suggest that she is any different from other young women of her age. She stresses that she has never lived in a gilded cage, protected from the realities of life; her mother has made sure of that. She is also quite genuinely amazed when someone suggests to her that she cannot possibly have had a normal family life, when palaces and castles have been open to her since the day of her birth. She wonders how can people be so stupid as to imagine that her grandmother goes around all day wearing a crown and refusing to enjoy some of the mundane pleasure of life just like everyone else. As she once put it, her grandmother may be Queen, and spend a lot of her time shaking hands, but that is just the family business.

If the Queen had any reservations about the way Princess Anne was bringing up her children, she was wise enough to say nothing, and anyway, Anne refused to be influenced by anyone's opinion. She knew how she wanted to raise her son and daughter and said, 'If you start down that road there's no end to it. You must do what you think is best for your child.' This was why, when first Peter and then Zara reached school age, they were not educated at home by a private governess, as the Queen and her sister, Princess Margaret, were, but at a local school.

By the time Zara was old enough, her parents decided she would attend the local nursery school, Scout Hut Nursery, in the village of Minchinhampton, less than a mile from Gatcombe, for a year. Anne had asked the Headmistress not to single out Zara as someone special, which proved to be an unnecessary request. The headmistress said, 'I treat Zara just like all the others. She is a lovely little girl – and just like any other child of her age she can be a rascal. She has made lots of friends and is very popular and she really enjoys learning.' Her mother asked Zara what were her favourite lessons. She replied they were the same as everyone else's: music and movement. When she was five, she moved a short distance to Blue Boys School for a very short period and then on to Beaudesert Park pre-preparatory school, also in the village, where she remained for three years from 1986–89. There is a story circulated around Minchinhampton that when the children at one of the village schools were asked by their teacher what their parents did for a living, as some replied with the usual sort of answer, Zara apparently said her Daddy rode horses all day, while Mummy went out and met people and shook their hands. Out of the mouths of babes, and all perfectly true of course.

When Zara came home from school, her mother was never too busy or tired to spend time with her and she often helped her with her homework, saying, 'To try to help my children to read was actually very difficult. I was concerned that I was doing them a disfavour, because my logic worked differently from theirs.' Whatever assistance Peter and Zara received from their mother, it soon became clear that neither was a natural academic. In Zara's case, what happened to her later in life proved that this was to be no handicap.

By the time Zara was settled at school, there was no need for a full-time nanny at Gatcombe and Pat Moss left. Her replacement was Sarah Minty, who was not a traditional nanny in that she helped around the house when the children were at school and also enjoyed doing some work on the farm. Zara loved being brought up in a farming environment and she enthusiastically joined in haymaking in the summer holidays, and learned to drive a tractor before she could legally drive a car. It was a close and loving family that gave her – and Peter – an all-important base of stability and security that stayed with them until adulthood. Mark had grown up just a few miles from Gatcombe, so his boyhood friends helped to make the Phillips circle close-knit and comfortable.

Being brought up in the country, Zara was introduced to field sports at an early age. Both she and her brother would accompany their parents to the Gatcombe shooting days, and again this caused criticism from the anti-blood sports campaigners. On one occasion, Zara was helping to pick up the dead birds that had been shot by the grown-ups when she found one that hadn't been killed outright but was lying in agony. The only way she knew how to put it out of its misery was to stamp on its head – and even this did not kill it. The following day headlines appeared screaming: ANNE'S GIRL STOMPS ON PHEASANT'S HEAD! Zara was upset at first, as she had thought she was being kind in trying to end the bird's life painlessly, but soon realised that this was all part of country life, and if one is going to attend shooting parties, there will inevitably be occasions when grouse, pheasants or rabbits have to be despatched in what seems to be a callous method if they are not killed by the first shot. Similarly, when she first learned to ride competently, she was allowed to join the local hunt. In those days there was not the organised antagonism that preceded the introduction of anti-hunting legislation in Britain, but there were pockets of protestors who always turned up when the riders and their followers gathered. They were all fairly good-humoured and there wasn't the anger and outright hatred that occurred later. No person or animal was injured in any protest and Zara and her parents (her cousins, William and Harry, also hunted, along with their father, but not their mother, as the Princess of Wales had fallen off a horse when she was a young girl and disliked the idea of hunting anyway) enjoyed their weekly outings with their friends in the area around Gatcombe.

One way in which Anne and Mark differed from other Royal parents was that they insisted on including their children when they spent weekends at horse trials or country fairs. They always took Peter and Zara with them, and it was during one of these outings that the children discovered, to their mother's amusement, that they shared her dislike of the media. Wherever they went, the 'Ratpack' of Royal reporters and photographers nearly always followed them, and Peter and Zara soon learned to show their displeasure at the constant scrutiny with gestures and shouting at them. Of course, that was exactly what the reporters were hoping for as it made good stories and picture captions for the next day's papers. The children were learning how difficult it was to live an ordinary life as members of the Royal Family. Princess Anne had admitted that 'there is a constant battle with priorities' between being a wife and mother and a working Princess. The former, becoming used to being called 'darling' or 'mummy' at home, the latter, accepting that people who meet you will bow or curtsey and refer to you as 'Your Royal Highness'. She also said that in those early years of her children's lives, being a mother made it very hard to concentrate on her public duties when the usual childhood ailments meant she felt she should be with Peter and Zara at a time when she was obliged to undertake an official engagement.

Zara was introduced to the various 'must-attend' Royal functions at an early age and she was always seen with the rest of the family when they went to Clarence House to wish Queen Elizabeth, the Queen Mother a Happy Birthday. As they gathered outside the house, where the Queen Mother lived for over half a century, for the ritual picture on her 91st birthday, the waiting crowd was amused to see that the Queen, Princess Anne and Zara were wearing nearly identical dresses, and all looked as if they had been made from curtain material.

In the summer of 1989, Zara's parents announced that they were to separate after nearly sixteen years of marriage. Zara was eight at the time. Unlike some children of divorced couples, for Zara the separation and subsequent divorce did not have a negative effect on her life as a child. A few months after the announcement, she was enrolled at Port Regis Preparatory School in Shaftsbury, Dorset, as a boarder. The school, founded in 1881 in London, moved to its present location in 1947, and is set in 150 acres of magnificent parkland. The fees for boarders are currently over £6,000 a term. Zara's mother and father felt that this school, combined with her early schooling at Beaudesert Park, would give her a decent grounding in learning to mix with 'ordinary' boys and girls of her own age, and at both schools Zara was accepted on equal terms by her fellow pupils. Fortunately, children are not as stupid as adults can be when it comes to social levels; they haven't yet learned to discriminate because of class or upbringing. Nobody allowed Zara to behave as Royalty, neither teachers nor pupils, not that she tried. Her mother's insistence on bringing her up as a normal girl paid dividends right from the word go. She was always a determined and self-willed child, but that had nothing to do with being the granddaughter of the Queen, or the daughter of a Princess (though, perhaps as her mother shared the same character-istics, it may have been in the genes).

The only time it might have seemed strange to the other boys and girls at Port Regis was at holiday time. When the others chatted about where they had been – Spain or Portugal with their parents for a couple of weeks, perhaps – Zara was able to tell them all about spending the summer at Balmoral Castle with Granny and Grandpapa, the Queen and Prince Philip. But even then, she had learned not to say too much about her Royal relations.

Zara had no problem with being sent away to boarding school at such an early age. But even if she had objected, it would have made no difference. Anne and Mark, with the Queen's approval, had decided that was the best thing for their daughter; her opinion simply didn't come into it. There was nothing cruel or unusual in their decision; it was just the natural extension of her early education, to prepare her for the next stage of her life. Princess Anne had been sent away to school herself and liked it from the very beginning. But as she once told me, 'It wouldn't have made the slightest bit of difference if I had bawled my eyes out. I was going and that was that.' When Prince Charles went away to school for the first time, he *did* cry bitterly and had to be forcibly torn from his nanny's arms. He never got over his misery and was often found sobbing into his pillow while at school.

Whenever a senior member of the Royal Family is seen out and about, armed police bodyguards always accompany them. With their immaculate clothes and highly polished shoes, they are sometimes mistaken for secret service agents – with a glamorous James Bond image. In fact, they are not detectives, but members of the uniform branch, wearing plain clothes. They do get a special clothing allowance, so they can merge with ambassadors and diplomats at Royal functions, but they are definitely not MI5. And when the Queen is seen riding in one of the State coaches to and from the Palace of Westmin-ster for the State Opening of Parliament, she is attended by two footmen seated on the back of the coach. However, only one is a real coachman; the other is a police officer, wearing the full State uniform of a Palace footman. He is always the one on the left side of the coach, so he can reach his weapon more easily. The Palace now has a number of female protection officers who are as equally well qualified as their male counterparts and when I asked one of them what her reaction would be if I got in the way of her performing her protection duties, her reply was succinct and to the point. 'I would shoot you,' she said.

Princess Anne has always had a team of armed police officers to guard her, and Zara was often seen in the grounds of Gatcombe, or other places, being carried on the shoulders of one of them. To the casual onlooker, they might have been taken for an uncle, or at least a close friend of the family. But when I asked one policeman, who worked with the Princess Royal for more than twenty years, what the relationship was like his reply put paid to that myth. He said they were treated as just another piece of furniture, perhaps even less so, as furniture was more valuable than they were. The children had had it instilled in them practically from birth that if one of the officers left today, another would take his place tomorrow. There was no closeness between either of the Phillips' children and their 'minders'. The protection officers were ordered by their superiors not to become involved with the children and the Princess certainly never encouraged any familiarity on either side. Press comment that they were some sort of surrogate fathers was clearly very wide of the mark.

The late Sir Peter Gibbs was private secretary to the Princess Royal for more than eighteen years and probably knew her better than any other non-family member. He was never in any doubt about his position, saying that Royalty was like a large picture frame with the family permanently installed in it, and that while many people passed by it over the years, none was allowed to remain. He added that lots of men and women imagined they enjoyed a special relationship with the Royal Family, but they soon discovered that the moment they 'fell off the twig' it was as if they had never been there in the first place.

The only servants who do occupy the thoughts of their Royal principals after they have left are some of the nannies and nurses. The Queen held her nanny, the redoubtable Bobo McDonald, in such esteem that, long after Bobo had retired, she was provided with a suite of rooms immediately above Her Majesty's own rooms in Buckingham Palace, where the Queen would visit her every day without fail. Bobo was the only person outside the Royal Family who was permitted to use the diminutive 'Lillibet' when addressing the Queen.

Princess Anne was much closer to Zara than she was to Peter. Anne was rarely seen at weekend horse shows without her daughter in tow and the Queen, who was obviously delighted to have a granddaughter, took her to the Royal Windsor Horse Show, where they were seen walking with the Queen holding Zara's hand. This raised a few eyebrows, as Her Majesty was never pictured in physical contact with anyone, even her own children when they were young. She was mistakenly said to possess a cold nature, which was far from the truth. The Queen is a warm, affectionate woman who loves children, but because of her position, she rarely shows any emotion in public. But one or two people who have engaged Her Majesty in conversation in recent years have found to their delight that a sure way of attracting her attention is to mention her grandchildren. Her face lights up and she loves to talk about them all and also to ask the person she is talking to about their grandchildren, if they are of a certain age. Prince William, as eventual heir to the throne, occupies a special place within the Royal Family, and naturally most of the attention is focussed on him, but the Queen has a very soft spot for Zara and throughout her life she has taken particular interest in her progress and welfare. Zara used to write to her when she was away at school and the Queen always replied in her own hand; she still does when they correspond. And no one could have been more delighted

or excited than Granny when Zara won her world championship.

Princess Anne blatantly flouted the rules regarding her
children on a number of occasions when it suited her,
including one particular Ladies Day at Royal Ascot in 1989.
The inviolable rule is that under no circumstances are children
allowed in the Royal Enclosure. Princess Anne, who was fully
aware of the rule, deliberately ignored it and paraded Zara,
who was then about eight years old, up and down the
enclosure wearing a brightly coloured spotted dress with a
straw hat and carrying a miniature handbag. Other people in
the enclosure remarked that the child looked extremely
precocious and pleased with herself. If the Queen noticed this
serious breach of protocol (and she must have known, as her
permission would have been needed before Zara could be
brought in) she was courteous enough not to mention it, and
neither did any of the Ascot officials. They were obeying the
unwritten rule, which is that the Royals may not always be
right, but they are never wrong. Someone who worked at
Gatcombe at the time said that although Zara was a normal
little girl and usually fun to have around, she could be a 'bossy
little madam' on occasions. There were several occasions
when Zara and her mother had violent disagreements, usually
over some trivial matter, and as they are so alike, they ended
up shouting and screaming at each other at the top of their
voices. The staff at Gatcombe soon learned to recognise the
signs that a row was brewing and kept out of the way. But
Zara and Princess Anne share one very pleasant characteristic:
neither sulks, so once the shouting matches were over, it was
all sweetness and light – until the next time. It was quite
amazing that even when Zara was still a young child, it was a
case of 'like mother, like daughter'. They were, and remain, so
alike it is uncanny, so if anyone wants to know what Zara will
be like in 30 years time, they only need look at her mother.

After several years at Port Regis, Zara went up to Scotland,
to attend Gordonstoun in Morayshire. The school was
founded by the German educationist Kurt Hahn, and had

been attended by the Duke of Edinburgh (when it was based in Germany) and his three sons, Charles, Andrew and Edward. Anne went to Benenden in Kent because at that time Gordonstoun had not become co-educational. It did so in 1972. Andrew and Edward enjoyed Gordonstoun; Charles hated it, which is partly why Princes William and Harry were sent to Eton (although the main reasons were that Princess Diana didn't want her children that far away from home and the Queen felt it would be better if William was nearer Windsor Castle so she could see him at weekends for a little tutoring in constitutional history).

Zara was thirteen when she arrived at the school, by which time the strict Spartan regime of early morning cold baths, summer and winter, had ended, much to her relief. It was still an establishment that encouraged self-sufficiency and many of the activities took place out-of-doors in the Scottish Highlands in all winds and weathers. It was the ideal place to toughen up youngsters.

It was in 1933 that Dr Kurt Hahn, Headmaster of Salem School in Germany, the forerunner of Gordonstoun, decided to move to the north of Scotland, after he had stood up to the Nazi regime and been advised that his name was on a list of 'undesirables'. At first, there were only a handful of boys in the school and Dr Hahn encountered many problems, including having to evacuate the entire school to mid-Wales during the Second World War, and finding, when they returned, that a fire had all but destroyed Gordonstoun House in the meantime. But with patronage from wealthy families and the support of the Duke of Edinburgh, the school went from strength to strength, until, by the time Zara joined, they had some nine boarding houses, a preparatory school and a junior school.

Fees at Gordonstoun are currently £7,572 a term, rising to £8,054 a term for sixth formers. The Junior School charges £5,088 a term. However, the school does have a scholarship system for outstanding pupils who might have difficulty in paying the standard fees. Zara, however, did not fall into that category.

One of the things that Zara particularly liked about Gordonstoun was that the school was well used to coping with pupils of many nationalities and from all walks of life, so, once again, as at her first schools, she found that being a member of the most famous family in the land was neither a hindrance nor an advantage. If she had wanted to, she could have taken her horse to Gordonstoun, but she decided not to. She felt there were enough activities available without adding equestrianism. And anyway, she could always pop across to Balmoral at weekends and ride one of the Queen's horses if she felt like it.

It was during one of these weekends that Zara invited one of her fellow students to join her at Balmoral. The young lady, who was from Holland, was just about the only person in the school who didn't know who Zara's family were, so when she was asked to 'pop over to my Granny's place with me', she had no idea that Granny was the Queen and that her 'place' was Balmoral Castle. When they arrived at the castle, they were admitted by a liveried footman who didn't raise an eyebrow at the sight of two young girls wearing jeans and T-shirts and carrying their overnight clothes in canvas hold-alls. Zara's friend was shown to a magnificent room where a maid unpacked for her and when the two girls joined the Queen and Prince Philip for tea, they were warmly welcomed. The Dutch girl said later that she had never had such a relaxing couple of days.

The philosophy of Gordonstoun is summed up in their school charter, which states: 'A Gordonstoun education prepares students for a full and active role as international citizens in a changing world.' As a member of the Royal Family, Zara had always been comfortable in the company of people of all nationalities, so Gordonstoun held few surprises for her in that respect. She made many friends from different countries while at the school, and most of them have remained in touch since.

During Zara's teenage years at Gordonstoun, her mother found she had to ride out a number of adolescent storms. When Zara had her tongue pierced for £35 at a tattoo parlour in Elgin, near Gordonstoun, she triggered a spate of news headlines, particularly when she revealed the piercing to members of her family at Prince Charles's 50th birthday. There was even a story, reported in the press at the time, that Zara had been caught with friends trying to sneak into the boys' dormitory at Gordonstoun, which was, of course, forbidden. Whether there was any truth in the story is debatable, but regardless, Zara's navel exposing and drinking in local pubs all attracted attention. Anne took it all in her stride. She and Zara often used to argue – and they still do, perhaps because they are so much alike. But whereas, in recent years, Zara has come to realise how privileged she is because of her Royal lineage, and so makes allowances for the media, Anne will never make any concessions. She can seem haughty and appears thoroughly regal at all times, where Zara is deliberately approachable and friendly in an effort to counteract the public image of a distant Royalty.

By her own admission, Zara is not an academic, but she knew that if she was to be able to progress to university, she needed the necessary educational qualifications, so she buckled down to her studies and managed GCSE exams and, two years later, sufficient A-levels to obtain a place at Exeter, one of the best universities in England, to study for a diploma in equine physiotherapy.

Before she took up her place at Exeter, Zara decided to take a gap year. She spent it, as so many young people do, in seeing the world. She travelled to Jamaica and Hawaii, and spent three months in New Zealand and Australia. In Sydney, she had plenty of introductions from friends of her parents, and stayed with two of them during her visit. She took on a number of jobs, just to get work experience, and says the best was when she became a stagehand for an Australian production of the musical, *The King and I*. She loved the atmosphere backstage, but wasn't tempted to try her luck before the footlights. She even worked for three months as a 'gofer' in a public relations agency in Sydney, which should have warned her about what can happen when spin doctors and journalists get together to sell a story.

Her time in Australia wasn't all work, of course, and she was seen having fun on the beaches with a variety of young men, all heavily tanned and muscled. Her informal style of dress attracted attention even then. The Aussies loved seeing her in her low-slung shorts, T-shirts and bikinis. It was the first time any of them had seen a member of the British Royal Family dressed so casually, and they loved it. In return Zara loved Australia. She adored the sunshine, the surfing and the fact that nearly everybody she met there was as sports mad as she was. News of her antics got back home when she started to appear in the tabloids Down Under. Pictures appeared of her allegedly sunbathing topless – in fact they were not of her at all, and were so blurred that no one could have identified her even if they had been. It was significant that not a single newspaper in Britain published the pictures.

Zara also tried bungee jumping (she couldn't refuse a challenge) and enjoyed the nightclubs and fashionable restaurants Sydney had to offer. She found the city to be vibrant and informal, and she loved the outdoor café society. After the comparative dullness of New Zealand, where it seemed that everything closed at six o'clock, Australia had a great appeal for the teenage Royal, with its round-the-clock entertainment and laid back attitude to life. But she was fairly circumspect at all times, remembering that anything she did would immediately be reported on and inevitably seen by Buckingham Palace. So, although she went out on a few dates, it was usually in the company of a party of other young people, never alone with a man. Her name was linked with several sports stars, including a New Zealand All Black (and much later with a British racing driver), and it was said that she fell for a doctor's son, Will Marien, in Sydney, and shortly afterwards began seeing Angus Murray, who was head boy at Australia's oldest private school, Kings College. But nothing serious emerged and it appeared that these were mainly tabloid elaborations. She knew the danger of being caught with someone so far from home and the mileage the newspapers would get out of such a story, so she was very careful to avoid the pitfalls.

Zara was aware that she had a half-sister living in New Zealand. Felicity Tonkin was born to her father and a woman he had known in 1985, well before his divorce from Zara's mother (Zara also has another half-sister, Stephanie Phillips, the daughter of Mark and his second wife Sandy). The sisters did not, however, meet during Zara's time in Australia.

Zara was nineteen when she returned to Britain to take up her place at the University of Exeter, where she studied physiotherapy, specialising, not surprisingly, in equine physiotherapy. It was a subject she would come to value in the years to follow. She also took a short course of three months at the University of Wales in Cardiff in 2001 in order to qualify as a sports masseuse.

It was while she was still at university that Zara decided to have a go at making a name for herself in eventing. She said later it was because her A-level results were not as good as she had hoped, but even then she was competing regularly and when the horse Toytown came along, there was only one way for her to go. That meant forgetting everything else and concentrating on reaching the top, and to do that she had to devote all her energies, and most of her time, to riding.

After leaving university, Zara started hitting the headlines for all the wrong reasons when in December 2000, while driving her Land Rover near Bourton-on-the-Water in Gloucestershire, she narrowly escaped serious injury after the vehicle turned over in a ditch. The papers made out she was at fault, but no charges were brought, she passed the mandatory breathalyser test, and she continued to drive – at times perhaps a little recklessly through the narrow country roads. Zara loves speed and she has occasionally found herself in trouble over her car, not always when it is moving. Two years ago, in January 2005, a newspaper published a photograph of her parked car with an out-of-date tax disc. Even if the tax had been paid, the fact that a current disc was not displayed was an offence and could have cost her a fine and penalty points on her driving licence. As she already had nine penalties at the time, a further three, taking her to twelve, would have meant a driving ban. Being a member of the Royal

Family would have made no difference, apart from the fact that the case would have made headlines.

Zara's car accident happened at about the time she was beginning her first serious relationship – with the leading National Hunt jockey Richard Johnson. It was a relationship that would give her some of the happiest moments of her life to date, and also propel her into the spotlight on more occasions than she might have wanted.

3 THE 'NON-ROYAL' ROYAL

Zara Phillips belongs to what has been described by some as the most dysfunctional and emotionally retarded family in the land, a description she would vehemently deny. But the family has experienced divorces, separations, adulterous love affairs (with even the Queen's sister openly conducting an affair with a man twenty years her junior while she was still married), illegitimate children and allegations of murder and conspiracy. There have been so many lurid stories in the press during the Queen's reign that, as unblemished as her own life has been, it would have taken a sizeable rainforest to provide the world's newspapers with the newsprint they have used.

The Queen and Prince Philip have four married children, with three of them divorced, and one, the heir to the throne, involved in one of the most scandalous love affairs in living memory when he admitted on television that he had committed adultery with the wife of a brother officer in the army, an offence that is normally punishable by a court martial. His ex-wife accused him of not being suitable as the next monarch. She then died in the most tragic circumstances in an incident that is still clouded in mystery. Eight years later, he married his mistress and in what was said to be a cynical public relations damage limitation exercise, gave her the use of one of his subsidiary titles, Duchess of Cornwall, instead of the legal style to which she is entitled as his wife: Princess of Wales.

His affair with a woman who was vilified as the person directly responsible for the break-up of his first marriage caused major constitutional problems for the Queen. Many Commonwealth leaders, particularly in those countries that do not believe in divorce, came to feel the Prince of Wales may not be the ideal candidate as Head of the Commonwealth when his mother eventually dies.

In another matrimonial controversy, Her Majesty's second son, Prince Andrew, Duke of York, found out that his wife was involved with her 'financial adviser', and photographs of her topless in the south of France appeared in the newspapers on a morning that they were both staying as guests of the Queen at Balmoral, causing secret amusement to some members of the family but acute embarrassment to the Queen. Prince Andrew and his wife, Sarah Ferguson (or 'Fergie' as she is widely known), then divorced, but remain on friendly terms.

Zara's parents' marriage lasted just under sixteen years before they too separated in 1989, when she was eight years old. Mark and Anne felt their marriage wasn't working and decided to end it. He later married his American second wife, Sandy, with whom he had a daughter. The Princess Royal went on to marry one of her mother's servants, Tim Laurence, and Anne and Tim and Mark and Sandy now all live happily on the Gatcombe Estate in a highly civilised manner.

This then is the family into which Zara was born.

Anne and Mark were divorced in April 1992, three years after they had separated. Eight months later, on 12 December, the marriage took place between the Princess Royal (as she had then become) and Commander Timothy Laurence RN. The wedding was held at Crathie Parish Church just outside Balmoral Castle under the auspices of the Church of Scotland. The venue was chosen because the church in Scotland has a more relaxed attitude to the remarriage of a divorced person than the Church of England. When the wedding plans were first announced, some old timers in the Palace were dismayed. As equerry to the Queen for three years, from 1986–89, Tim had carried out the duties of a trusted servant without giving a hint that he was involved with his boss's daughter. He was even awarded the MVO, the most junior level of the Royal Victoria Order – the Queen's personal order of chivalry and given only for outstanding service to her or a member of her family. Senior members of the Household remarked that it was not for *that* kind of service that medals were intended. One reluctant guest at the wedding was the bride's grandmother, Queen Elizabeth, the Queen Mother, who attended even though she privately agreed with the stand of the Church of England. She felt her absence would have attracted more attention than her presence and so attended out of family solidarity.

Zara adores her father and was said practically to ignore her stepfather when she was going through that 'difficult' stage as a teenager. Since then, Tim has been wise enough not to try to take the place of Mark; he is more like a big brother to Zara than a stepfather. They get on well together now but do not see all that much of each other during the working week as Tim spends from Monday to Friday in London. He also accompanies the Princess on some of her overseas tours when his duties allow.

Tim has prospered in his naval career since he married into the Royal Family and has risen from being a mere Lieutenant Commander when he first joined the Royal Household, to his exalted present rank of Rear Admiral. Tim began his sea-going career as 'Season' officer on board the Royal Yacht *Britannia*, which is where he first met his future wife. Season officers, as the title implies, were employed only during the summer months when the Royal Family were likely to be on board. Now with the navy rapidly reducing the number of ships in the fleet, opportunities for sea-going appointments are few and far between and competition is fierce. So Tim is chained to a desk in Whitehall, through no fault of his own. Unless he gets a senior posting, it looks as if he will remain on dry land for some years to come, which is frustrating for a keen officer who only joined in order to go to sea.

The Mountbatten-Windsors (for that is the name under which Princess Anne was married to Mark Phillips) are headed by Prince Philip, Duke of Edinburgh, surely the only 86-year-old man in the world who still has to walk the mandatory two steps behind his wife whenever they appear in public. While Elizabeth II is Head of State and Queen Regnant, no one in the family is in any doubt that Philip runs the show when it comes to family matters. Until recently, he summoned his four children to Balmoral, where they gathered at Craigowan House (where Charles and Diana loved to stay, but where Camilla refuses to set foot) once a year to hear their father's comments about their performance during the previous twelve months. It was not always a pleasant experience. Philip has never been one to mince his words and often when he let rip, the children, especially Charles, were nearly reduced to tears. Philip used to set each of them targets for the coming year and if they did not achieve them, he wanted to know why. Excuses were not acceptable.

The Queen was not invited to the round table discussions at Balmoral. Neither was any member of the Royal Household, and no minutes were recorded. But Prince Philip took copious notes and would check them the following year to see if his orders had been carried out. Now that the children are all in middle age, the formal annual reviews have stopped, but Philip still asks searching questions if and when he believes one of them is slipping, and if satisfactory answers are not forthcoming, his language is not for delicate ears.

Philip has been described as a distant and forbidding father, particularly towards his three sons. Yet, when they were small, he spent many hours happily playing with them and friends who were around at the time said he was a very affectionate parent. Both Philip and the Queen were naturally deeply disappointed when Charles and Diana divorced and Philip is said to be concerned over what has been called Charles's main fault – his indecisiveness. Members of the

Household have been heard to murmur that Charles does not inspire confidence in the future. Andrew is the playboy of the family, whose marriage to Sarah Ferguson went hopelessly wrong, though by fighting with great distinction in the Falklands Campaign in 1982, when he was a helicopter pilot in the Royal Navy, he secured a special place in his parents' affections, as they both love anything to do with service life. Their third son, Edward, has settled down after failing to complete his initial training course in the Royal Marines, which, surprisingly, disappointed and angered his mother more than his father. Now he has married successfully, and his wife, the Countess of Wessex, has lived down the early disasters of their marriage, when she was still working in public relations and fell for a confidence trick when a reporter, posing as an Arab sheik, talked her into promising access to the Royal Family in return for a lucrative contract. This was in 2001 and her indiscreet remarks about public figures included the Prime Minister, Tony Blair, who she called 'President Blair' and his wife, Cherie, who she described as 'horrid, absolutely horrid' caused something of a stir. The Countess even made disparaging remarks about her mother-in-law and Queen Elizabeth, the Queen Mother, and suggested that Prince Charles and Camilla Parker Bowles were at the top of the list of the most unpopular people in Britain. The resulting headlines brought acute embarrassment to the family and Prince Philip was understandably furious. Luckily for the Countess the Royal Family felt they could not add yet another scandal to those already revealed by publicly rebuking her, so she escaped with a private dressing-down from the Duke of Edinburgh, which must have been a sight to behold. Edward now undertakes public duties, specialising in the Duke of Edinburgh's Award Scheme, and his and his wife's rehabilitation within the family seems secure. Prince Philip never criticises Edward; in fact, he speaks in very affectionate terms about his youngest child, something he rarely does about the others, even his clear favourite.

The only one of his children that Philip never finds fault with is his daughter. Princess Anne has never put a foot wrong in her public life and she is rightly regarded as the hardest-working member of the Royal Family. She regularly tops the league table of Royal engagements (sometimes tying with her father) and in one poll it was clear that many people believed she would be preferable to Charles as the next sovereign.

Anne and her father share many characteristics: they both loathe the media, both speak their minds openly, and in Anne's view her father can do no wrong. He returns the compliment and courtiers have been heard to say that Anne is the son Philip wishes he had had. Where Charles is the incurable romantic of the Royal Family, Anne is the no-nonsense pragmatist.

Prince Philip is believed to have never forgiven his eldest son for the way he thought he betrayed the rest of the family by cooperating with Jonathan Dimbleby in a remarkable television programme and authorised biography that revealed his innermost thoughts and feelings. When Prince Charles told his biographer that he had an unhappy childhood and his parents didn't understand him, not only his father, but also his siblings were furious. Princess Anne said later that she didn't recognise the family he was describing. As far as she was concerned, they had all had a normal upbringing and felt their mother and father were loving and caring parents. At the same time, the children understood the limitations and responsibilities their parents laboured under, so they didn't expect to see all that much of them. When your mother is also your sovereign, it cannot be a totally exclusive relationship. Allowances have to be made.

Any parent with four children, three of whom are divorced, must question where they went wrong. If, like Her Majesty, that parent is also Supreme Governor of the Church of England, and a committed Christian to boot, the questions must cause acute anguish. For generations, the British Royal Family has been held up as the perfect example of happy and contented family. The idea of divorce was unthinkable, even as recently as when the Queen came to the throne in 1952. No divorced person was permitted to enter the Royal Enclosure at Ascot and nobody who had been through the divorce courts, even as an 'innocent' party, was allowed to serve as a member of the Queen's Household. How things have changed. Not only was the Queen's own sister divorced, but also, if the rules about the Household were still in existence, Buckingham Palace staff would be decimated.

Of course, attitudes have changed in the last half-century and Zara and her brother have grown up with parents who divorced and remarried happily. All four – mother and stepfather, and father and stepmother – live in harmony within a mile or two of each other. It's a very civilised arrangement. Mark Phillips and his ex-wife even organise commercial shooting parties together on the Gatcombe Estate. No one is quite sure what Tim's role is when these take place, but Zara has bought her own partner, Mike Tindall, a shotgun so he can join in.

Divorce didn't mean an acrimonious row over custody or visiting rights for Zara's parents. They all get on well and Zara and Peter certainly do not appear to have suffered because of the family break-up. Princess Anne and Mark were in total agreement on one point – that the children must come first – and so they tried to work out what was best for them. They never argued in front of Peter and Zara and all the discussions about their upbringing, including their education, ended in mutual agreement. Mark would have liked Peter in particular to follow in his footsteps and go to Marlborough, but Prince Philip – and Princess Anne – convinced him that Gordonstoun would suit him better.

Anne's creed was that a child's home life had more influence in later life than school and she was determined that Peter and Zara should enjoy a happy home. Their parents may not have been the perfect married couple, but they were the ideal mother and father. Zara was once asked if there were any problems because of the divorce. She was mystified by the question. She couldn't understand why there should be any difficulties. Anyway, when she was at school, she was part of the majority, as many of the other pupils came from 'broken' homes.

It might be argued that the Royal Family has at last moved into the twenty-first century with their marital problems, and become more in line with the rest of the nation. So far we haven't seen a civil partnership taking place, but the Queen does now allow homosexual members of her staff to bring their partners to the annual Christmas dance, even if she has let it be known that she prefers not to see them dancing together.

Because Peter Phillips rarely features in the media, he is often described as the 'invisible Royal'. It is a description he is happy to have applied; it is entirely his choice not to be newsworthy (though when he marries, it will still make headlines). Peter decided when he left Gordonstoun that he did not want to take up competitive equestrianism; he did have the option, and he is a more than competent rider, but that wasn't what he wanted to do and the subsequent focus of attention on Zara suits him down to the ground.

What is not generally known outside the family is how close Peter and Zara are. Because he lives and works mainly in London, and his job in Formula One motor racing takes him all over the world, he does not see Zara as often as they both would like. But they keep in touch constantly and there is an incredibly strong bond between them. Mutual friends who have known them all their lives, say it all goes back to their schooldays. When Zara started at Port Regis preparatory school in Dorset, Peter was already there and he looked out for his little sister. Similarly, when Zara joined him at Gordonstoun, Peter had already established himself as a rising sports star, playing in the school 1st XV rugby side, which led to a 'cap' for Scotland. He was very popular with his peers and he made sure that Zara had an easier entry into the public school system than might have been the case if she had been on her own.

More recently, no one took more pleasure and pride in Zara's success in the European and World Championships than her brother. He is not a demonstrative young man – neither are their parents openly demonstrative – but he was with her in Aachen, and he was almost in tears when she passed the finishing line to take the title. They both know that if either of them needed a shoulder to lean on, the other would be there for them; it's that sort of relationship.

When the Princess Royal is at home, she often sees Zara at some time during the day, but most weekdays see her leaving the house early in the morning and not returning until late evening, by which time Zara is either working in the yard, or relaxing in her own home with Mike. Zara knows that she can talk to her mother about anything, more than she is able to confide in her father. While Zara physically resembles her mother, she has also inherited many of the emotional traits of the Princess Royal. She is down to earth, with a salty sense of humour and a smattering of 'stable' language that is common among equestrian folk. She doesn't swear for effect; it just comes out naturally when she is with contemporaries. She also possesses an engaging laugh, and enjoys a dirty joke or two, just like her mother. Besides their obvious mutual interest in all things to do with horses, Zara and her mother have other strong similarities: both can be abrasive and never avoid confrontation, with others or with each other. In the past this has led to stand-up rows between the two, particularly when Zara was living at home. It is said that one of the reasons why Anne converted the barn on the estate for Zara to live in, instead of giving her space back in the big house where there was plenty of room, was that neither fancied the idea of living together in such close proximity.

One of the differences between Zara and her mother is that the Princess Royal hates shopping, and did even when she was a teenager. She cannot remember the last time she entered a shop when she wasn't on duty. And neither does she like spending money; to her frugality is a virtue. Zara thinks shopping is OK as long as it is done locally and does not entail a drag up to London. Her mother's proud boast is that a good suit can last for years, so she has hers made with extra long hems so they can be let down and taken up according to what is fashionable. I once mentioned to her that the outfit she was wearing seemed familiar. She replied that it ought to be as she had had it made 25 years ago.

*　　*　　*

British Royalty does not take kindly to outsiders, and by that they mean anyone not 'born to the purple'. They have occasionally had to allow commoners into the fold when seeking new blood to be married into the family, as the pool of willing and available European Royal sons and daughters dries up. But the newcomers, even aristocrats such as Lady Diana Spencer, whose family had served the monarchy for centuries, soon find out that they are admitted on sufferance and are never treated as 'one of us'. King George VI liked to refer to his immediate family as 'The Firm', meaning himself, his wife and their two daughters, Elizabeth and Margaret. His theory was that by keeping 'The Firm' compact and exclusive, there was less likelihood of trouble. And he has been proved right, over and over again.

The Royals have also traditionally discouraged familiarity with outsiders. Nobody outside her immediate family addresses the Princess Royal in any way other than Your Royal Highness or Ma'am (to rhyme with ham, not smarm), and the very idea of calling the Prince of Wales 'Charlie', or even Charles, would simply not occur to anyone, even those who were at school with him fifty years ago and have kept in touch ever since. He discourages any form of familiarity, and one of his oldest school friends once said that Charles was born middle-aged. Of course, it is not all Prince Charles's fault. He grew up in an age when Royalty was expected to behave in a manner different from ordinary people. His nursemaids and nannies impressed on him that he was special, and so did his mother, knowing that his destiny was to be King one day. He disclosed as an adult that he had been desperately unhappy during his childhood; whereas his sister said she couldn't understand how he could claim that as she and her other brothers all felt they had enjoyed a glorious upbringing.

Prince William also knows how to keep people at arm's length but his brother, Harry, is much more approachable, and male and female friends have often been heard in pubs and nightclubs using his first name. Of course, William, like his father, is a future King and has been made aware of his unique position practically from birth, so his actions are not because he is deliberately being unfriendly but because he knows that if he encourages too much informality, it could come back to haunt him in the years to come. The Queen has instilled this reticence in her grandson from an early age, knowing that when he becomes sovereign it will mean, among other problems, he will be isolated from nearly everyone except his immediate family.

Considering she is the granddaughter of the reigning monarch, and the great-granddaughter of the last King/Emperor (until India gained its independence in 1947), Zara lives a comparatively normal life. She can go wherever she likes, with whomever she chooses and, to a large extent, behave as any other young woman of her age and class. The only difference is that she has a direct line to the Queen and says, 'I often call her and tell her what my horse has been up to.' So, whether it is dysfunctional or not, this is one young woman who appears to love her family and enjoys being part of it. And she can't see what all the fuss is about.

The relationship between Anne and her daughter is extraordinarily close, but so is that between Anne and her own mother. When Michael Fagan broke into Buckingham Palace and Her Majesty woke up in the morning to find what must be every woman's nightmare – a strange man sitting on the end of her bed, dripping blood – it was to her daughter that the Queen turned for comfort. She didn't discuss the matter with any of her closest friends of her own age, or with any of her Ladies-in-Waiting, who had worked for her for many years; not even her mother or sister. It was only Anne that she wanted and Anne was there for her.

Zara has a special feeling for her grandmother; they share the same interests, mainly horses of course, and the Queen is kept fully informed of everything that Zara is doing. In Zara's eyes, Granny can do no wrong and the feeling is reciprocated. The Princess Royal did not have the same affinity with *her* grandmother, Queen Elizabeth, the Queen Mother, for some years. This was partly because the Queen Mother favoured Prince Charles to the exclusion of all her other grandchildren.

He was the unchallenged favourite and he returned her affection in full measure. When she died, at the age of 101, he was devastated and could not be consoled for days. The Princess once revealed her regrets at not having 'discovered' her grandmother until comparatively late in her life, saying, 'The Queen Mother is a wonderful family person and when I was a child and up to my teens, I don't think I went along with the family bit. So my appreciation of my grandmother probably developed later than anybody else's.'

For her own part, Zara enjoyed the company of her great-grandmother. Along with William and Harry, she loved to go to Clarence House or up to Birkhall in Scotland in the summer and call in to see how Gan-Gan, as they called Queen Elizabeth, was getting on. What Zara really appreciated about the Queen Mother was that she was completely non-judgemental. Nothing seemed to faze her; when she found out about Prince Charles's affair with Camilla Parker Bowles, she accepted the fact, as long as the monarchy wasn't threatened. And it was only when Diana revealed the affair and went public about her opinion of Charles and his alleged unsuitability to become King that Her Majesty turned against her former granddaughter-in-law. She once confided to a Lady-in-Waiting that she could understand Charles needing a Camilla in his life, as many men needed someone like her from time to time, as long as it didn't harm the monarchy.

When William and Zara used to visit her, they would regale her with tales of what they were up to at university, and the more risqué the stories, the better she liked to hear them. She even offered them both a sip of champagne long before they were legally allowed to drink, saying it was a good introduction to one of the finer things in life – and anyway, she considered champagne to be medicinal. When Zara had her tongue pierced and appeared with a stud in her navel, she knew that Gan-Gan wouldn't be offended, and she wasn't. In fact, she was intrigued to find out how the piercing was carried out, but didn't think it would suit her.

When the Queen Mother died, Zara was visibly upset, but not grief-stricken as Prince Charles was. The death had been expected for some time as Her Majesty was a great age, and when it happens so peacefully to a woman who is over one hundred years old, it is difficult to be shocked or to feel anything but a deep sadness. There certainly wasn't the wave of emotion and grief that struck the nation in 1997 when Diana, Princess of Wales died so tragically.

Zara remembers her Gan-Gan with enormous affection and also viewed her Aunt Margo, the late Princess Margaret, as a misunderstood and tragic figure for whom she felt tremendous love and a great liking. She believed that Princess Margaret lived the life she wanted, and that is something Zara can identify with completely.

With all these different relationships within the family, the wonder is that Zara and Peter have matured into responsible and sensible adults with no airs and graces. It is a tribute to the down-to-earth attitude to parenting of the Princess Royal and Mark Phillips that their children are the nearest things to normal it is possible to be and remain members of the Royal Family.

Perhaps it all goes back to when they were very small children. When Zara attended primary school in Minchin-hampton, her mother insisted that she mix with the other children, and Zara made many friends, most of whom are the best of pals to this day. Zara used to compare notes with William when she was at Gordonstoun and he was at Eton. She couldn't believe that he had to wear a 'panic button' at all times in case of attack or attempted kidnapping, and she thought it was very funny when a couple of William's fellow pupils took the button off him and threw it in the Thames. Of course, she didn't realise then just how important it was for the eventual heir to the throne to be in constant contact with his protection officers until she found out how furious they were.

Zara soon began to understand there was little cause to envy her cousin, particularly when she heard that he had remarked how much he hated the thought of having his whole life programmed down to the last detail and that he would have no say in his own future. She sympathises with him. He will never know the freedom she takes for granted, so he is making the most of the years he has until he is crowned King.

Zara gets annoyed when people say the Mountbatten-Windsors are not a normal family, and cannot be because of the formality and protocol that surrounds everything to do with Royalty. Zara reckons that the myth has grown through misinformed comments from people who are on the outside of the Royal circle, and it is their perceptions that have become the accepted opinions of many through repeated stories in the media. If they could only see her extended family as she does, when they all get together, doing the things everyone else does, perhaps they would realise how ordinary they really are. Zara is ultra-protective of the family name and will not allow jokes to be made about any of her Royal relations. She has some regrets that her early exploits – tongue-piercing, unsuitable relationships and public rows – have, at times, reflected badly on the Royal Family. But she believes that, far from being the most dysfunctional family in the land, the Mountbatten-Windsors are fully functional. They know they are different and cannot behave in public as other people do. But in the final analysis, because they are such a tight-knit and self-supporting unit, they know they can rely on each other completely. They also believe that they neither need nor want anyone outside the family. Which is why, when one of them marries a commoner, they are admitted only on sufferance, and never allowed to forget the fact.

4 HOME SWEET HOME

Z ara grew up in a beautiful home in an idyllic setting. Gatcombe is a secluded, stone-built mansion with stables, garages and plenty of outbuildings to hide in and play. It is surrounded by acres of rolling countryside, where the children were free and safe to wander all day long. Dogs and horses were very much in evidence, and the dogs were never restricted to being kept out of doors. They had – and still have – the run of the house. These days the furniture has that comfortable, lived-in look that comes only with 'old money'. There's no suggestion that a member of the *'nouveaux riche'* lives here. It is probably like a thousand other country houses in Britain, with nothing of the stately home about it. Nothing looks brand new and even when Zara was born, 26 years ago, the place still had that old-fashioned, not-quite-shabby, but knocked-about appearance that takes generations to achieve.

Just before Zara's brother, Peter, was born, Princess Anne and Mark Phillips had moved into the house, which was bought for them by the Queen in 1976 from the former Home Secretary, 'Rab' Butler, whose family home it had been for generations. Mark Phillips became the official Master of Gatcombe on 29 September 1976, but not its owner. The eighteenth-century mansion and its 733 acres had been on the market for some time – and not lived in for more than ten years – and the seller later said that Her Majesty had driven a hard bargain. The price was never revealed but is believed to have been in the region of £500,000 (the price of an average four-bedroomed semi in Ealing these days), driven down from the original asking price of nearer £700,000. With prime agricultural land in the county at that time fetching around £1,000 an acre, the house came for nothing. Today the estate is worth at least ten times the original amount.

The Queen did not hand over the deeds to her daughter and son-in-law; Royalty does not work like that where property is concerned. They were given the right to live there, but only at the Queen's pleasure, which meant the ownership remained in her hands, so that in the event of a divorce (which, of course, later happened) there was no question of a division of community property. The same principle applied when Prince Andrew married Sarah Ferguson and they wanted a new house. Nothing suitable could be found around Windsor, their preferred area, so Her Majesty built them a brand new property (cruelly nicknamed 'Southyork' in reference to the garish house occupied by the Ewing family in the American television series, *Dallas*) for a reported £5 million. But again, Andrew and his bride did not have the house registered in their names. It still belonged to the Queen. Her Majesty never cared for Sunninghill Park, the official name of the property, and it was finally sold to a private buyer in April 2007 for a reported £7 million – £3 million less than the original asking price.

As Gatcombe is the official residence of the Princess Royal (she also has a free 'Grace and Favour' apartment in St James's Palace across the road from her office in Buckingham Palace, in what used to be the Palace schoolroom), the cost of its upkeep, which is substantial, comes from part of the Civil List, but anything to do with the stables or farm (500 arable acres are attached to the estate), in other words the private side, is paid by the Princess herself. A specialist company based in Cambridge handles the administration of the farm. The property is very convenient for the Princess, as it is only 112 miles from Buckingham Palace and near to Kemble railway station. She often uses the train to travel to London, getting her connection to Paddington at Swindon, and even though the stationmaster is aware that she is travelling, he does not make any special arrangements. She travels first-class, but in an ordinary carriage with the other passengers. The only concession to her status is that her car is allowed to wait on the concourse at Paddington for her arrival.

Anne and Mark had been looking for a home for months before they found Gatcombe. They later said they felt they had seen every house in the Home Counties – and further afield – and had just about given up when Gatcombe was brought to their attention. When Princess Anne (as she was then) first saw the house it was a daunting sight, needing rewiring, replumbing and complete decoration. The electrics in particular were in a volatile and dangerous condition. The air of neglect gave little hint of what a graceful and elegant home it was to become when it was restored to its former glory.

What persuaded Anne and Mark that this was the house for them was the magnificent setting: rolling valleys and deep woodlands – and even a 'folly' built by a former owner. Princess Anne once told me that the 'folly' was the clincher as far as she was concerned. It was the 'wow' factor that made Gatcombe the right place for her.

Before the young couple could move into the house, there were major structural alterations that needed to be done. The bedrooms were all confined to the back of the house, where there is no view and the outlook is dark and forbidding. The bathrooms were at the front, and so they all had to be demolished and moved to the rear. Every time the builders overcame one problem, they encountered yet another.

Anne and Mark must have had tremendous faith in the project and a great deal of imagination, not to mention money, to get the house in habitable condition. They took out a mortgage for the repairs, but, of course, the Queen had already bought the house and land so there were no crippling interest payments to be made on these. Shortly after the Queen bought Gatcombe, a neighbour approached Mark and offered him Aston Farm, which adjoined the estate, together with its additional 500 acres. Mark and Anne knew it made commercial sense to extend their estate but when Mark sought a mortgage from several banks and building societies, he was turned down for a number of reasons, one of which was that he didn't have a steady source of income. He would have obtained the money eventually, but there were no definite offers forthcoming immediately. When the Queen heard of their problems, through her daughter, she immediately offered to finance the purchase, bought the farm outright (obviously she did not need a mortgage) and leased it back to the couple. Mark and his second wife, Sandy, now live there.

When Anne and Mark were divorced in 1991, it was agreed that, as part of the divorce settlement, Aston Farm would be held in trust and become the sole property of Peter and Zara, with Mark being allowed to live there for the rest of his life. So he and his wife reside at the pleasure of his children, and in time, Peter and Zara will become very wealthy landowners indeed.

Back at Gatcombe, the first thing the builders did was to gut the entire first floor, moving the bedrooms to the front where they would have superb views. Then they set about changing the attics on the top floor. Under its original owners, who employed an army of domestic servants, the attics were a warren of tiny, dark rooms. Princess Anne wanted a separate, self-contained nursery floor and this was constructed out of the old attics, turning them into a light suite of bedrooms, bathrooms, a sitting room and a kitchen. (When the children grew up and left for boarding school, the nursery was converted once again, this time into a suite to be used by guests staying with the Princess and her husband.) But even though it was self-contained, the children were never restricted to the nursery floor of Gatcombe. They had the run of the house and nowhere was there any sign of the sort of grandeur one might have associated with the homes of members of the Royal Family. No rooms were sacrosanct. The Princess was determined that her home would have a 'lived-in' look and visitors are still likely to share armchairs or sofas with dogs, who roam quite freely about the place. Gatcombe Park then was the ideal home in which to bring up children.

Furnishing a house the size of Gatcombe would have been no easy matter for the average young couple, but as the daughter of the sovereign, Princess Anne had a choice of many beautiful items from the Royal Collection. Nothing new was bought, but there were plenty of wedding presents that proved suitable for different rooms. There was a need for paintings and other works of art to decorate the walls of the hall, drawing room and dining room and once again, the Royal Collection offered a selection. These were all politely returned. Instead the paintings that adorn the walls at Gatcombe all reflect the interest of the Princess Royal in sporting matters. There are pictures with an equestrian theme and others showing her passion for boats.

Many people who are guests in Royal residences complain (quietly) that they are never warm enough. That doesn't happen at Gatcombe. The central heating system is efficient and economical and, as the Princess loves an open fire, the drawing room always has a huge log fire burning throughout the autumn and winter months. There is an abundance of timber on the estate and logs are piled up in the fireplace, replenished every day by one of the staff.

It's very easy to miss Gatcombe. As you leave the village of Minchinhampton in Gloucestershire on the country road that runs due east, the entrance to the estate is on the right hand side, just about a mile from the village. There is no sign to indicate the name of the house or its location, so unless you know where you are going, or are accompanied by someone who does, you could easily pass it. Beyond the entrance to the property there is a long, winding, tree-lined drive about half a mile long, which has to be negotiated with great care as it is deliberately kept difficult to drive for security reasons, with overhanging laurel bushes making it a dark thoroughfare even in daylight.

Before you see the house itself, the driveway divides, with a signpost directing all traffic to the right, round the rear of the property. There is a security post skilfully designed to blend in with its woodland surroundings and which is manned permanently, night and day, by policemen of the Gloucestershire constabulary, not officers of 'A' Division of the Metropolitan Police, who form the Royalty and Diplomatic Protection Department, which is responsible for providing security for members of the Royal Family. Nobody gets past this post without an invitation. But once the security guards have verified that you are expected and checked the number of your vehicle, always requesting politely but firmly that you remain in your vehicle, you are allowed to drive around to the front of the house, alongside the Princess Royal's Bentley or one of the estate Land Rovers. Zara was taught to drive by her mother on the private roads that criss-cross Gatcombe before she was allowed out onto the public highway with 'L' plates.

The first impression one gets, is that the house is not nearly as large as it looks in pictures. While it is beautifully proportioned, the illusion of size is because of the magnificent conservatory that is attached to the house on the left-hand side as you look at the building. The glass conservatory was added to the house in the nineteenth century and it has been estimated that to build it today – if you could find the craftsmen – would cost well over £50,000.

As you enter the front door of the house, you immediately find yourself in a stone-flagged hall that still boasts, at the rear, a large old-fashioned rocking horse, once used as a plaything for Peter and Zara, now a great talking point for visitors. On one side of the hall is an ancient table on which lie copies of *Horse and Hound*, *The Field* and *Riding Monthly*, giving a clue to the interests of the tenants, while underneath is a water-bowl kept filled for the dogs that are given free rein in the house.

To the left of the hall is the formal drawing room where official guests are received and beyond this is the Princess Royal's sitting room with an elegant bow window that looks out over the grounds. It is here that Her Royal Highness likes to sit at her desk, working on personal correspondence and also on her speeches (unlike other members of her family, she writes all her own speeches). On the right of the hall is the dining room, which is used only when she is entertaining. It is a pleasant, formal room containing a magnificent table that can comfortably accommodate up to ten guests for dinner. When no guests are expected, the Princess and her husband usually eat off trays in the sitting room. The days when Royalty dressed formally for dinner every evening, even when alone, are long gone. Even the Queen and Prince Philip now eat informally, whereas when King George V and Queen Mary were living at Buckingham Palace, he wore a formal frock coat and the Garter Star every night, while Queen Mary was never seen without a full-length gown and diamond tiara. The informality of life at Court today would, no doubt, horrify the Queen's grandfather, or even her own parents and her late sister. Princess Margaret was the last of the Royals to insist on formal wear for dinner at Kensington Palace and she was once invited to a friend's house for dinner and was completely bemused to find a napkin ring beside her plate. When she was told what it was intended for, she couldn't understand that some people used the same napkin for more than one meal. It didn't happen like that in her home.

Gatcombe then was home to Zara for the first 21 years of her life – before she moved out to live with Richard Johnson, and then moved back onto the estate to live with rugby international Mike Tindall. Around the main house are a number of buildings that are used for a variety of purposes: garages, stables, security offices and barns that are perfect for conversion to living quarters. But Zara did not move into her new home at Gatcombe just to accommodate Mike. She and the Princess Royal were already converting the Cotswold stone building her mother had made available. The original intention was for Zara to live there alone after she had broken up with Richard Johnson, as she didn't want to move back in with Mum. It was just a happy coincidence that the place was ready to live in when Zara and Mike decided to move in together.

Home for the couple has been described as a 'cottage' on the Princess Royal's estate. In reality, it is a converted barn that has been turned into a substantial two-bedroom house with plenty of room for Zara and her 6ft 2in, sixteen-stone lover to spread out. To help them keep fit they have installed a mini-gym where each spends a couple of hours every day working on the machines in order to build up the strength they both need for their respective sports. In estate agents' parlance, the property would be described as a 'des res' (a very desirable residence) and if the house were put on the open market, it would probably fetch around £500,000, the same price the entire Gatcombe estate cost the Queen when she bought it for Zara's parents in 1976. But Zara and Mike do not own the property; neither do they pay any rent. As with the main Gatcombe estate, the deeds remain with the Queen during her lifetime.

As the Queen is the landlady of Gatcombe (and Aston Farm, just two miles from the main house, where Mark Phillips and his second wife, Sandy, live) it is said Zara had to have her permission before she could ask her boyfriend to move in with her. Surely this was the only time in history that a sovereign had been petitioned to allow a granddaughter to 'live in sin'? Zara will also require the sovereign's consent before she can marry, otherwise she will have to give up her place in the Line of Succession, not that there's too much chance of her ever becoming Queen Zara I, as her position at eleventh leaves her some way down the ladder.

The repairs to Gatcombe are paid for by the Princess Royal and the conversion costs of the barn where Zara lives, believed to cost around £200,000, were also met by Her Royal Highness. Zara and Mike really do have the best of both worlds. They live in one of the nicest parts of the country, with security paid by the taxpayer, and they are far from the prying eyes – or long lenses – of cameramen and photographers. It's just as well, as Mike has installed a luxury hot tub outside the house where he and Zara like to spend a few hours at weekends, particularly after Mike has played a tough match for Gloucester. He justifies the expense of the hot tub – which cost £17,000 – by claiming they need its curative powers after the bumps and bruises they suffer doing what is now for both of them full-time jobs as sports people. But he has no need to justify his purchase. It was his own money that bought it, so why not enjoy it, for whatever reason?

Speaking about his purchase of the high-tech hot tub, Mike said, 'It's big enough for eight people but the main reason I bought it was to help ease my muscles after training. It has jets that massage my whole body and it helps me to sleep better – although the water can get as hot as 40°C.' The tub is equipped with a state-of-the-art waterproof television, DVD and stereo system. If Mike and Zara wanted to get the money back that they paid for the hot tub, they could ring up any tabloid newspaper picture editor, who would be delighted to offer them twice that amount for a photograph of them sitting in it together.

Zara and Mike see the Princess Royal almost every day, if she is not away on Royal duties, and she often invites them to join her for dinner if she knows they do not have a punishing schedule the next morning. Mark will also pop over most days, if he is not in some distant part of the world working on his coaching and course-designing activities.

Life is very comfortable for Zara and Mike and also for her parents. They enjoy each other's company and share the same tastes in sport. Whether the young couple will remain at Gatcombe if they marry is anyone's guess. The house they have at the moment suits them beautifully, but no independent man wants to start married life living practically under the same roof as his mother-in-law – even if she is Royal.

5 A RIGHT ROYAL RIDER

'I've wanted to go to the Olympics ever since I could ride,' Zara says. 'It's special to be selected for your country and I enjoy being part of a team. It would be better to ride in the Olympics or to win a medal for your country than to ride at Badminton. I now realise how much Mum and Dad's achievements mean . . .'

Three day eventing is a dangerous sport. Riders have been killed on the fearsome cross-country courses that make up one third of the sport, and serious injuries frequently occur. Minor injuries are commonplace and no rider, world champions included, has escaped without some sort of mishap.

Zara was knocked unconscious when one of her horses, Ardfield Magic Star, threw her two years ago during a competition at Lulworth Castle in Dorset. She and the horse both landed on their heads after failing to take a fence, and Zara was completely out of it until paramedics brought her round.

She was taken to hospital in Dorchester to have a check-up, where an X-ray showed she had broken no bones, but her left shoulder needed to be strapped up before she was discharged and driven home by her mother, who had been with her throughout the ordeal. Buckingham Palace was flooded with enquiries about Zara's condition and they said she had been given the all clear. Zara had been lucky this time, as the previous owner of the horse had died after falling off him. Zara made light of the fall, as her mother had done when she was knocked unconscious herself during the Montreal Olympic Games, but it could just as easily have been much worse – riders have been killed or paralysed for life.

As the daughter of two Olympic competitors, one of whom won a team gold medal in 1972 and a silver in 1988, and the other of whom completed the notorious cross-country course at Montreal in 1976, Zara would seem to have been born to be a champion – or bred for the job. Mark Phillips was part of the British Olympic Team and Princess Anne became European Three Day Event Champion in 1971, when she was just 21 years old.

Zara once said she did not want to equal her parents' achievements, 'I want to do better than them.' She certainly started well in her aim to reach the top. Like all successful riders, Zara had started out in Young Riders, with her early successes including victory in the Under-25 Championship at Bramham, followed by an individual silver medal in the European Young Riders Championship in 2002, a competition her father reckoned she could have won.

Everyone who has ever had anything to do with horses says it is like attaching a tap to your wallet. The expense is enormous and you never stop paying out. Feed, stabling, vets' bills, horseboxes – if you are going in for serious competition, the sky's the limit. It is an outrageously expensive sport. One horse is never enough. You have to have a string so that if your star performer suffers an injury or loses form, there is always another to take his place. To train and keep a horse for major three day events means you won't see much change out of £20,000 a year, and there's virtually no chance of getting your money back. With Zara's string of horses, plus her grooms and other costs, the total annual budget is not far short of half a million pounds, and the financial rewards are few, unlike horseracing, where, if you own a succession of winners, you actually may show a profit at the end of the season. But even here the truly successful owners are limited to a mere handful, to whom racing is an expensive pastime, rather than a source of income. Even the Queen, who has owned many winners in her lifetime, including winners of most of the Classics, except the Derby, has a limited budget, and she rarely shows a profit. With three day eventing now an international sport that involves extensive travel overseas, the costs rise every year, and nobody, including the Queen's granddaughter, could manage without the help of commercial sponsors.

Eventing is the toughest of all equestrian disciplines and comprises dressage, cross-country and show-jumping. Its roots go back to the early nineteenth century when it began as a form of endurance riding in the French cavalry, known as the *raids militaire*. The endurance tests included, in 1892, a ride from Berlin to Vienna, a total of 360 miles, which the winner completed in 71 hours and 26 minutes. This was the forerunner of the three day events we know today.

The first competition to resemble the events we have these days was held in 1902, but eventing was not introduced into the Olympic Games until 10 years later, in 1912. At those first Games, only military officers on active duty were permitted to take part, and it wasn't until 1924, at the Paris Olympics, that male civilians were allowed to participate. Non-commissioned army personnel were banned from the competition until 1956, and women were not allowed to enter until as recently as 1964. Today, equestrian sports are the only Olympic events in which men and women compete on equal terms against each other.

It wasn't until 1971, when Princess Anne entered the sport seriously, that three day eventing began to attract much notice. Prior to this, it had been a comparatively minor Cinderella sport restricted largely to military riders and farmers' sons and daughters. But when the Princess began to take part, the press and subsequently the general public started to show an interest. Of course, at that time Princess Anne was the Royal they all loved to hate because of her uncompromising attitude. She refused to accommodate photographers and reporters, saying 'I don't do stunts' when asked to pose for special pictures on a foreign tour. So when she appeared at Badminton, one of the elite international three day events, over 100 photographers waited at the water jump on the cross-country course, all willing her to fall in so they could get a picture of her going head first into the water. In fact, she was dumped in the lake only once during her entire career, but the incident was recorded by 150 photographers, and live television cameras, and was seen in newspapers and magazines all over the world. Of course, if she had been just any other rider, it wouldn't even have made the back pages, but she wasn't and she was realistic enough to accept that it was part of the price she had to pay for being Royal.

The old adage that there is no such thing as bad publicity held good for eventing as Princess Anne showed her mettle and continued to achieve great success, culminating in victory in the European Three Day Event Championship at Burghley in 1971, the year she was also voted Sports Personality of the Year.

Outwardly, Princess Anne has never given any indication of being nervous – and neither does Zara – but shortly after winning the European crown she admitted that, 'For three nights I didn't sleep much before Burghley.' Looking back on that event, it is difficult to remember that among the other riders she beat were Richard Meade, arguably Britain's best ever three day event competitor with four Olympic gold medals to his credit, the then reigning World Champion, Mary Gordon-Watson (who, some years later, would enter the sporting history books by becoming the first lady jockey in Britain, and who was later joined as a jockey by Princess Anne racing in the Queen's colours), and a member of the official British team, Debbie West.

Princess Anne was not included in the official British team, although she had achieved fifth place earlier that year at Badminton. The selectors took the unusual step of justifying her exclusion by issuing a public statement:

The selectors were greatly impressed by Princess Anne's performance at Badminton. However, since this was the first international competition for both of them [Anne and her horse Doublet] and in view of the very large number of experienced combinations available, it was not thought advisable to include Her Royal Highness in the shortlist from which the team will be chosen.

However, the selectors hedged their bets and she was invited to compete as an individual; history has recorded what happened next. So, it was largely due to Princess Anne's participation that the sport in which her daughter now shines came to be recognised as an important part of the international calendar.

The three phases of three day events have origins of purely practical and military use. Dressage demonstrated the horse's ability to perform on the parade ground, without vocal commands, where obedience and elegance was the key. Cross-country was a test of stamina and courage over difficult terrain, required if a charger was used for a long, arduous march across unfamiliar country, while the show-jumping sought to prove that the animal was still fit and sound after a particularly difficult cross-country gallop. The dressage phase is always held on the first day when the audience is usually made up of very knowledgeable riders and supporters, and comprises an exact sequence of movements ridden in an enclosed area, all carried out in complete silence. Every time a rider speaks he or she loses valuable points. The judges look for balance, rhythm and suppleness coupled with obedience and total harmony between rider and horse. Each movement in the test is scored out of ten. The competitors are allowed two errors: the first costs them two marks, the second, four marks and the third means elimination. Both rider and horse are required to be immaculately turned out, with the riding attire for dressage being a black or navy coat, shirt, stock tie and pin. Gloves are also required, as are black dress boots. Top hats are optional, but are usually worn, and the rule for breeches is that they should be white. This section of the competition is a demonstration of mutual understanding between horse and rider, and of the rider's skill in schooling the horse.

On the second day comes what is easily the most popular phase for spectators – and in most cases for riders also – the cross-country circuit. This is a gruelling test of speed and endurance for both horse and rider, demonstrating not only the courage of rider and horse but also their complete trust in each other. The course covers several miles and has to be completed in a set time. Riders and horses must attempt to clear a large number of fixed obstacles of varying degrees of difficulty on their way around the course. The fences are constructed of heavy materials, such as telegraph poles, stone walls and tree trunks, and are based on obstacles one would normally encounter in the countryside. They are unlike those in the show-jumping ring, which are so lightweight they are displaced almost as soon as they are touched. If a rider hits a fence during the cross-country circuit, it's the horse and rider that give way, not the fence. Prior to taking part in this section, all the riders 'walk the course', measuring the distance between fences and the height of the obstacles. One doesn't have to jump every fence. There is always an easier way around, but that means losing time, so all the leading riders attempt to go by the shortest route, cutting corners, and trying to stay seated at the water jump, where most of the spectators – and press – are always waiting, hoping to see one of the stars going headfirst into the lake. The phase is timed and any rider finishing after the allotted time incurs 0.4 penalties for every second they are late. If a horse refuses at a fence it results in 20 penalty points; a second refusal at the same fence means 40 penalties and a third refusal at the same fence means elimination. If a rider falls off his or her horse, they incur 65 penalties and a second fall again means elimination from the competition.

It's not difficult to understand why the audience appeal of three day events is concentrated on this middle day. Everyone watches the speed and endurance test, with its 47 bone-shattering fences, constructed so that they look as if it would take an earthquake registering at least 8 on the Richter scale to make them even tremble, never mind collapse, and designed with devilish and infinite complexity. Many viewers watch not hoping that the leading exponents of the sport complete a clear round in record time, but praying that the horse – all half a tonne of it – will come to a sudden, shuddering halt, propelling its rider over or into the fence, or better still, making him perform a neat swallow dive into the lake in a tangle of blood, sweat, flesh and bone. That is how we get our vicarious thrills: from seeing, from the safety of the sidelines, someone else risking getting hurt. It's been acknowledged many times that a spectacular fall at the water jump is good for the sport, as it generates more publicity than all the clear rounds put together.

The cross-country phase often sees injuries to both horse and rider. Thankfully these are not usually serious, but occasionally horses have had to be put down after failing to clear a fence, and riders have been killed. Because the cross-country course can cause serious injuries, each rider is required to wear a medical armband giving his or her blood group and any other medical details, and they must wear a protective body-vest and an approved riding helmet. Before the last day and the show-jumping finale, there is also a very strict veterinary inspection to ensure that the animals are fit to continue. The riders are expected to declare themselves able to go on.

Eventers all agree that most competitions are won and lost on the speed and endurance test, but if there are several riders who are closely placed at the start of the final day, it can make for an exciting finish.

The show-jumping section nearly always takes place on a Sunday afternoon, and by this time the favourites have usually emerged. If two or three are leading after the first two sections, they normally go last, and it is from these that the winner inevitably comes. Again, riders race against the clock, but the coloured fences they encounter here in no way compare with those seen in show-jumping competitions proper. They are lighter and lower and consist of elements that can easily be dislodged, unlike the solid cross-country obstacles, and are really no more than a test of the horse's fitness and stamina after the previous day's gruelling ordeal. This phase is also timed, with penalties being awarded for every second over the official time. Each fence that is knocked down means four penalty points, as does a first refusal. A second refusal in the whole round means eight penalties.

Three day events are the ultimate challenge to horse and rider. The ability to complete each section in the required time and without incurring penalty points requires total concentration throughout the competition, and if any of those cavalry officers of 200 years ago were to suddenly arrive on the scene today, they might be pleasantly surprised at the way the sport they started has developed without losing any of its charm, appeal or rigorous discipline. Britain has traditionally been in the forefront of eventing, but New Zealand, Germany, Italy and the United States have all produced successful teams and individuals, winning many medals at World Championship and Olympic level.

This then was the sport that Zara entered when she decided to make equestrianism her profession. So why did Zara choose this most demanding of disciplines? The decision to pursue eventing as a full-time occupation, as opposed to merely treating it as a rich girl's part-time hobby, was taken quite deliberately, and in the full knowledge of the amount of dedication and sheer hard work that was involved.

It is a tribute to Zara's natural ability and eagerness to learn that she so quickly got to grips with the basics of eventing. She was already a more than adequate horsewoman, but she had never before had to school and train her horses: that was a skill she needed to be taught. The discipline required was not only directed towards the horses, but also towards herself. A rigid training programme was worked out and Zara was forced to prepare herself as strictly as her mounts. The physical demands of eventing mean that a rider has to be in tip top condition, so Zara began working out with weights and she was given exercises to strengthen her thigh muscles and forearms. Obviously it all paid off in the end, but in those early days it took a lot of effort for her to get out of bed at the crack of dawn each morning, especially during the cold, frosty days of winter.

Of course, Zara's parents, both being former Olympic riders, were there to guide her and offer advice when she started, and being who she is – and who her grandmother is – opened many doors that would have remained firmly closed to other riders of her age. But Zara was determined to test herself against other competitors on equal terms, and she could not have chosen a better sport in which to try. Three day eventers are notoriously jealous of their own place in the sport and right from the beginning they were totally unconcerned about her Royal pedigree. They still are. None was going to give her any quarter because of the accident of her birth, and she never asked for any.

Zara was practically born in the saddle. She cannot remember a time when she could not ride. The grounds at Gatcombe Park are ideal for a young rider to learn to handle cross-country courses before venturing into open competition, and both Anne and Mark instilled in their daughter the discipline she needed to make her mark.

In an interview Mark Phillips gave in 2006, he described Zara's attitude when she first started competing. 'For years she was an absolute brat,' he said, and it took some time before she was willing to listen to her parents' advice. Nothing unusual in that. Every mother and father in the world has probably gone through the 'brat' period with his or her teenage offspring. Mark said she went through a phase when being told something by her dad wasn't easy. 'Then she came of an age when she realised that Dad is not completely stupid,' he said. After all, as coach to the American three day event team, Mark Phillips is one of the highest paid professionals in the game, and what the Americans were paying good money for, his daughter was getting for nothing. Added to that, Mark has impressive credentials as a rider, having won the prestigious Badminton Trials no fewer than four times, the only man to do so. (Lucinda Green, formerly Prior-Palmer, is the only woman to have won four times.)

Zara and her father often rubbed each other the wrong way when she was in training. Mark is not the sort of man who pays compliments easily and Zara once dubbed him 'Mr Negative' for what she thought was his lack of a positive attitude towards her. She was wrong there, as Mark found it much more productive to criticise her and point out where she was going wrong, than to praise her when she did something well. He knew she had the talent to succeed, and he also realised that to win she had to master her faults herself. Her main fault, in his view, was her lack of concentration. She could be brilliant in the early stages and then fall by the wayside simply by not paying enough attention. One of the things she objected to was that when she was being coached by her stepmother, Sandy, in dressage, Mark would occasionally stand around and make unhelpful comments. She was perfectly willing to accept his advice on cross-country and show-jumping, her weakest phase of eventing, but Sandy was, and is, the acknowledged expert in dressage, so Zara didn't want Dad interfering when they were working together. It was all pretty light-hearted bickering and, as Zara admits, Mark does know what he is talking about. The difficulty lay in separating the fact that he was her father from the fact that he was also one of the best trainers in the world. Zara also thinks her mother is more laid back than her father, and she shares more of Princess Anne's characteristics than Mark's. On occasion, Princess Anne would be around when things weren't going smoothly between Zara and her father, and she would sense that Zara was getting annoyed. The best thing she could do was to take Mark away until things cooled down.

Captain Mark Phillips has unique qualifications for coaching the successful USA three day event team, which he has done for the past fifteen years: he was twice an Olympic medallist, achieved numerous Badminton successes, and is

ex-husband of the woman who won the European Championship in 1971. The whole family is steeped in eventing. Added
to that, Mark is one of the leading course designers in the
world and would love to achieve the one ambition that has
eluded him as a designer. He wants to design an Olympic
three day event course. But at the present time he would not
even be considered for the job because of a possible 'conflict
of interest', both as coach to the United States team and, of
course, because he is Zara's father.

Speaking about eventing in general and Zara's performance
in particular, he emphasised that it is almost impossible to
compare the achievements of today with those when he and
Princess Anne were riding. He reckons every phase of eventing
is tougher today than 30 years ago. Technically, the dressage
is harder, the speed and endurance test is infinitely tougher,
and even the show-jumping, believed to be the easiest of the
phases, is much more difficult than it was. It may still not
compare with show-jumping proper, but it is still harder then
in the 1970s. Mark pointed out that the same applies in every
sport and that nothing stands still, with competitors now
fitter, keener and possessing a more professional approach.
Even in eventing, which is regarded as an amateur sport,
surely? Mark suggests saying that to a rider who is up at
dawn, mucking out and training and riding horses for up to
twelve or fourteen hours a day!

Concerning the elite image of eventing, Mark believes it is
not, and never has been, an exclusive sport. While it is
certainly expensive, at any trials you will still see someone
with an old Land Rover, pulling a trailer or horsebox, and
probably sleeping in it overnight because they cannot afford a
hotel or even a pub.

What about Zara's introduction to equestrianism and when
he first noticed there was real talent in his daughter? Like
many youngsters brought up in the country, both Peter and
Zara were lifted onto ponies when they were quite small,
but Zara didn't ride at school, and neither did Mark. It was
when she returned from her gap year in Australia that Zara
decided riding was what she wanted to do and so her father

had a good look at her potential. So what were the qualities he recognised? First of all, she was well-coordinated, which is vital, and she also had an inbuilt sense of balance, which was unusual in one as young as she was. The basic elements were there and so they built on that. Mark began to coach her in jumping and endurance.

What about Zara's attitude in those early days? She was not as driven as she has since become. She used to think things were OK, but Mark told her OK doesn't win. Good is good, better is better. Mark explained that one has to be prepared to work harder than the rest if you are going to get to the top, and that was her ambition right from the start. He told her, 'Is it easy? No. Is it tough? Yes.' Mark is not a great believer in luck. He reckons you make your own luck in this world.

What he is particularly proud of is the age at which Zara won two of the most prestigious titles in the world. She was by far the youngest member of the British team at the World Championships, and she is nowhere near her prime yet. It will take another six or seven years for her to reach, so the London Olympic Games in 2012 could easily be a realistic target: after all, she will still only be 31 then.

Once Zara decided that horses and eventing were to be the mainstay of her sporting life, she got down to the business of building a solid team around her and getting herself into the superb physical condition she knew she needed to be in if she was going to compete on equal terms with her peers. She realised, from her parents, that horses are no respecters of rank, and they soon know if the person sitting on their back is up to the job or not. Before her American-born stepmother returned from living in Germany and took over as dressage coach, Australian Andrew Hoy and his German wife, Bettina, both of whom are very successful international equestrians who compete as part of opposing national teams, had trained Zara. She began by competing at three day events up and down the country, with varying results, and by the time she was 21 she was moving into the higher echelons of Britain's young riders. Her father claims she could have won the European Young Riders Championship in 2002 if she had not had a fence down in the show-jumping, and that particular phase of the three-discipline competition has since been her bugbear. She even told her father that she couldn't 'f*****g' show-jump when she again had a fence down in a World Championship qualifier after being in the lead. He told her it was all in her head and she would just have to get on with it and forget all that nonsense about it being a jinx.

Zara soon became a familiar face on the equestrian scene and fairly rapidly established herself as a serious rival among her contemporaries. There is no particular snobbery in show-jumping and eventing, it's just that it is such a highly competitive business that those at the top fight hard to remain there, and do not have the time to notice anyone who does not appear to be an immediate threat.

Until Princess Anne emerged as Europe's top rider in 1971, even the country's leading show at Badminton was as much a social event as a sporting occasion and attracted only a few thousand visitors to the Duke of Beaufort's magnificent estate. Anne's success and the subsequent television coverage changed all that practically overnight, so that when Zara began there was already worldwide interest in the sport, and her presence added a further touch of glamour that did it no harm whatsoever.

But it was Princes Anne's success that propelled three day events into the public's awareness. With her single victory, she gave the sport its biggest ever boost. From being a minority sport supported by a few thousand hardy spectators, it would grow in popularity until it ranked, in television terms, with racing and athletics as a major crowd puller. Princess Anne deprecates her own part in the success of the sport, saying it would have happened anyway and that it was just a matter of time. But those who run eventing freely admit that had it not been for her involvement and the subsequent coverage by the media, it would probably still be confined to the wings of the world's sporting stage.

Of course, Zara's riding pedigree goes back much further than just her parents. On her father's side, her grandparents were horsey folk who hunted regularly, while on her mother's side, the Queen won her first major competition, carriage driving, at the Windsor Horse Show in 1948 – long before Prince Philip took up the sport. Today, even at the age of 80, Her Majesty still rides every morning when she is at Windsor or Sandringham, and she still infuriates the 'safety brigade' by refusing to wear a hard hat, preferring a soft, silk headscarf.

Zara's grandfather, Prince Philip, now 86, has had more influence than anyone else in the world on the way international equestrian sport has developed. He remains the longest-serving President of the International Equestrian Federation (FEI), the organisation he headed from 1964–1986, and it was he who founded the show-jumping World Cup. He created the rules for competitive driving and proved he could put his money where his mouth was as part of the British team that won the gold medal in 1980. Prince Philip's contribution to his sport was recognised in January 2007 when he was inducted into the British Horse Society's Equestrian Hall of Fame, where his name on the Roll of Honour is just behind that of his daughter, the Princess Royal, who had already been inducted. Zara has yet to be awarded this unique honour, but having won both European and World titles in successive years, her name must surely have been mentioned somewhere in the British Horse Society's hallowed halls.

If horses figure largely in the overall sporting picture of the Royal Family it is understandable. The tradition of equestrian excellence in Britain's Royalty is as established as the monarchy itself. The Queen was given her first pony at the age of three by her Uncle David, the future Duke of Windsor, when he was Prince of Wales. Both Prince Charles and Princess Anne started their riding careers before their fourth birthdays, as did Prince William and Prince Harry, and Peter and Zara Phillips were both lifted onto Smokey, their Shetland pony, and led around Gatcombe before they started at nursery school. Until Zara won her World Championship, her mother was the most successful sporting competitor in the Royal Family. And at the time of writing, Anne is still the only member of the family to have been chosen to represent Britain at the Olympic Games, when she competed in Montreal in 1976, a games at which the team won no medals. Those games are best remembered for the cross-country section, when Princess Anne fell heavily at the nineteenth fence and was knocked unconscious. She was badly concussed but remounted and finished the course – remembering nothing at all about it to this day – to become only the second British competitor to complete the section. The other finishing rider was Richard Meade, who came fourth. Zara hopes to be selected for the Olympics in Beijing in 2008, when the equestrian events are actually being held in the steamy atmosphere of Hong Kong. If she is chosen, she is determined to go one better than her parents and win an individual gold medal. Her father was awarded a team gold at the 1972 Munich Olympic Games, but never won an individual medal.

As Zara began to emerge as a competitor to be reckoned with, she realised that success was a double-edged sword. On the one hand it did focus attention on both herself and the sport, but there was also the danger of a backlash when one section of the press acclaimed her as the new 'golden girl' of eventing, and others said she was just a glamorous model in a hard hat who was trading on her family's reputation. While she accepted the attention of the media as part of the job, it did mean she was put under enormous pressure, unlike most of her contemporaries, who were allowed to train and compete without the unremitting glare of non-stop publicity. However, Zara is made of tough material. She was able to cope with everything the press could throw at her and because she has been in the public eye all her life, as the Queen's first granddaughter, she has learned not to let adverse comments bother her, or to let the compliments go to her head.

She is also a very driven, extremely competitive young woman who likes to win at everything she attempts. The idea of being a good loser simply does not appeal to her in the slightest. This attitude comes from her mother and father, who share the same feeling. When Anne and Mark were competing, coming second was just not an option. In fact, this is something all the leading sportsmen and women in the world have in common: they hate losing. That is why Zara became respected in eventing. Her fellow riders quickly realised she wasn't putting on airs and graces because of who she was, and she was a fearless rider who asked no quarter and certainly gave none.

As she and Catherine, her groom, travelled the length and breadth of the country in their state-of-the-art horsebox, they became familiar faces on the circuit and Zara was accepted as 'one of us' by the other competitors. Well, most of them anyway. There were still one or two who felt she was being treated differently because of her family background, but in the main no one took those complaints seriously and they soon faded away.

One difference between Zara and her mother is that when Princess Anne was competing she insisted on driving herself in the horsebox and never allowed anyone else to take the wheel. Even today, Her Royal Highness prefers to drive herself whenever she possibly can, particularly in the Royal Bentley. And, of course, an armed police protection officer always accompanied Anne, as has been the case ever since a man attempted to kidnap her in The Mall in 1974.

Unlike her mother, Zara usually leaves the driving to Catherine, while she snuggles down in the back of the horsebox, where they have comfortable bunks and a television set. She passed her Heavy Goods Vehicle driving test in April 2007 and so does hold a licence to drive the box (and indeed she regularly drove the vehicle on the private land around Gatcombe before passing her theory exam). But she doesn't mind being a passenger, so Catherine is probably going to be 'allowed' to continue to take on the bulk of the driving to and from horse trials. And, unlike her mother, Zara does not have a protection officer travelling with her. Neither she nor her brother is allocated police protection, as they are not considered to be prime targets at the present time.

One crucial element in Zara's rise to the top of equestrianism has been, of course, her horse. 'He's the biggest spoilt brat in the world. He stomps for attention and kisses and cuddles,' she once said. Zara could just as easily have been talking about her boyfriend, but her words were instead about Toytown, the horse that carried her to the top of the world in Aachen and helped to bring her the European Championship in Blenheim.

They say that in eventing the rider is only as good as his or her horse, and Zara has one of the best. Her mother had Doublet, on whom she won the European Championship in 1971 (and it was said that when Doublet broke a leg and had to be put down, it was the only time anyone had ever seen Anne shed tears), while Zara has Toytown.

Now thirteen years old, Toytown (who Zara calls Noddy after the famous Enid Blyton Toytown horse) was seven when he was spotted by Mark Phillips at a Pony Club event in 1999. Mark made an offer of £23,000 which was accepted and immediately the partnership between Zara and Toytown was forged and Zara was on her way.

Four people have equal shares in Toytown: the Queen, the Princess Royal, Mark Phillips and Zara, and they all have a special fondness for him. 'I guess he's a family favourite,' she says. 'He's got a huge character and thinks he's the best thing in the world, but he's a big baby and needs loads of attention. If I don't ride him first, he gets stroppy and bangs on the stable door. He goes mad at first when you ride him – he's like a big dog that needs exercising, but he's not an easy horse to ride.'

Before Mark bought Toytown, it was important that Zara approved, as she was the one who was going to ride him, and according to her it was love at first sight. Fortunately, Mark could see the potential in the horse and that there were still enough years left in him to achieve it.

The age-old question in equestrianism is this: who is the more important, horse or rider? There are those who say it is always the horse and that a merely average rider should do well on a brilliant horse. An equal number counter this argument, saying an outstanding rider can do great things with even a mediocre horse. There is never going to be agreement between the two schools of thought. However, nearly everyone agrees that Zara is an exceptionally fine horsewoman who has had the good fortune to be partnered by a fabulous horse in Toytown. Pippa Cuckson, former deputy editor of *Horse and Hound*, says, 'There is a wonderful *joie de vivre* about her riding, but she's very disciplined as well. She doesn't dictate to the horse. It's a partnership. Of course the horse has to be good, but so does the rider.'

Equestrian Olympian Richard Meade agrees. 'Toytown is a brilliant horse, but like so many with his qualities, not a very easy horse to ride. It takes someone with extraordinary talent and courage to get the best out of him and Zara did just that. When you have a horse as good as Toytown, it can look as if he is doing all the work and you simply have to hold on. It's a complete fallacy. Zara and Toytown are a wonderful combination with each needing the other equally.'

Toytown is a big horse, a chestnut who has the temperament of many big stars. He knows when Zara is feeling good on his back, and he can tell if she is having an off day. He likes to have a snooze in the late morning and gets irate if he is disturbed. But he comes alive on the big occasions and loves nothing more than to have an appreciative audience cheering him on. Noise doesn't bother him at all – in fact, the shouts of the crowd urging him on do just that. He responds to loud applause just like the star he is. His cross-country achievements are his main strengths, and the tougher the course, the more he seems to like it. Zara puts his occasional failings in the show-jumping ring down to laziness. Her father says it's *her* lack of concentration and reckons if she rides as she did in the World Championship, then she won't win an Olympic medal, which seems rather harsh considering she won the title in Aachen. What Mark meant was that standards advance all the time and Zara and Toytown would have to improve on their Aachen performance to maintain their winning ways. Mark is not the only one to say this; other experts in the equestrian field all believe that a winning performance one year does not guarantee success the following season. Work never stops.

When Zara first rode Toytown she knew there was a lot of work to be done if he was to realise the potential she and Mark believed he possessed. He was lazy but she knew he could be very good; just how good even she couldn't imagine at that time.

After winning the World Championships, Zara was swamped with awards and Toytown received a couple of his own. He was made the Petplan Equine Horse of the Year by the British Equestrian Writers' Association and at the London International Horse Show, just before Christmas 2006, he was named KBIS Equestrian Event Horse of the Year and was presented with the trophy in the ring at Olympia. Zara said she would take the trophy home and put it outside Toytown's stable door.

The biggest problem that Zara has when it comes to her riding is that all her eggs are in one basket. Toytown is the star of her stable, and even though she has one or two young horses who are coming along nicely, none is ready yet to take over Toytown's mantle. Red Baron is a good horse but he is eleven years old and in March this year, at the Land Rover Gatcombe Trials, Zara rode her newest acquisition, the twelve-year-old Glenbuck, formerly owned by her friend, the late Sherelle Duke. What Zara needs is another good horse or two to take the pressure off Toytown. Another injury like the one he suffered before the 2004 Olympic selection, when they were short-listed for the British team, would probably set her back a couple of seasons, and could easily be the end of Toytown's career – and she can well do without that.

Right from the start of Zara's career, she and Mark knew where they were going. The first target was the European crown and after that, the World Championship. We now know, of course, that in the space of twelve months she achieved both her ambitions and surpassed everything her mother and father had accomplished. So what has been the secret of her remarkable success so far and at such an early age? Well, in addition to a world-beating horse, she possesses a combination of determination, talent, shrewdness and an attractive willingness to learn from her own mistakes, or, as she puts it, 'When things go wrong, you can't blame the horse, because you are in control.' Conversely, while she is ready to listen to advice, she is not always prepared to follow it. But, as one of her colleagues puts it, 'She does sometimes have a tendency to feel she knows better than anyone else. Yet, as she is now World Champion, who can say she is wrong?'

6 LOVE LIFE (PART ONE)

R ichard Johnson is one of the most successful jump jockeys in Britain and Europe: 200 winners in a season, the youngest jockey to have ridden 100 winners in four consecutive seasons, and victory in the Cheltenham Gold Cup on Looks Like Trouble in 2000, have ensured that he can pick and choose his rides and made him financially independent. He is as well known in the racing world as any jockey, and better than most. His relationship with Zara Phillips is one of the best-documented affairs of recent years, and propelled him into a celebrity circus that went far beyond any sporting achievements.

Before he met Zara, his celebrity was confined to the racing community; afterwards everything he said and did became newsworthy to a much wider public. Photographs of them together appeared in newspapers and magazines throughout the world, and while Richard had been used to the sporting press reporting his riding successes and failures, he was totally unprepared for the avalanche of stories and column inches that descended on him once the media discovered he and Zara were a couple. The Queen's granddaughter and the champion jockey was the stuff that news editors' dreams are made of. Their turbulent, on-off love affair fed tabloid newspapers for the three years they were together, during two of which they lived together, and for months after they split in what was claimed to be an acrimonious separation, but which Richard says was perfectly amicable – they simply grew apart and decided to go their own ways.

Zara has never spoken about her break-up with Richard but he wrote an autobiography, published in 2002, in which he gave some details of the time they lived together and his version of the split. In a book of some 288 pages he devotes only 11 to Zara and if readers were anticipating salacious tittle-tattle about a scandalous Royal love affair, they were very disappointed. This was not a kiss-and-tell account of a Royal love story that went wrong. The chapter was discretion itself and Richard went out of his way to speak highly of his former lover, saying that, contrary to press reports, the parting was on the best of terms and he and Zara have remained good friends ever since. Press stories about the so-called inside revelations by 'close friends' of the couple about their stand-up rows, fisticuffs, screaming matches and Zara's tears and tantrums, are all anonymous, never attributed and can usually be found to be totally invented. It is true that Richard and Zara were both volatile young people; she had never had anyone stand up to her before she met Richard, while he, being a thoroughly modern jockey, was used to a lifestyle that was demanding in the extreme. His was also a career that meant exposure to the public and media, and in recent years other leading jockeys such as Frankie Dettori have become famous not only for their prowess in the saddle, but also for their flamboyant attitudes outside the racecourse. It's all showbusiness these days, a crazy merry-go-round of personalities and celebrities who are pursued by those who want to be seen in the company of anyone as long as they are famous for something.

Richard actually knew the Princess Royal before he met her daughter. The Princess used to keep several horses at Jackdaws Castle, the yard belonging to the late David Nicholson, known throughout the racing world as Duke. Princess Anne used to ride out for Duke when she started as a jockey, and she often said it was one of the happiest times of her life, sitting around the kitchen table having breakfast with the others lads after early morning stables. On more than one occasion I joined them and saw for myself the informality and camaraderie of the equestrian world. The conversation around the breakfast table was spontaneous and jolly, with no one waiting to be asked a question by the Princess. If anyone had something to say, they said it, and if they disagreed with her opinions they let her know in no uncertain terms. The language was a bit ripe too.

It was during a visit to Duke's yard that Richard Johnson first met the Princess Royal, little knowing, of course, that a short time later he would be living with her daughter. Richard remembers that everyone at the yard treated the Princess like anyone else, even though they all knew who she was. She didn't want any fuss, and she didn't get any. Jockeys, stable lads and trainers are like that; they are no respecters of rank, just ability.

Shortly after Richard began working for Duke Nicholson, Zara started riding out there as well, and this is where she met the man she was going to spend three years with. Zara was still at school at the time, and it was during her summer vacation from Gordonstoun that she began riding regularly at Jackdaws Castle. She was still in the middle of her A-level exams when she and Richard began to meet socially, but only with large groups of other young people around.

There were no romantic intentions on Zara's side then, and to be honest none on Richard's side either. He was 22, she was 18 and in the 1999/2000 racing season his star was very much in the ascendancy. Zara hadn't even started pursuing a riding career, so she was way behind him in the equestrian stakes. After successfully completing her A-levels in biology, geography and physical education, Zara headed off on her gap year abroad.

It was when she returned to the UK that things started to happen, but slowly at first. She and Richard used to meet for the odd drink in local pubs in the Cotswolds and then, at a party given by Duke Nicholson, they found themselves thrown together and spent the entire evening ignoring everyone else. From accounts of others at the party, it seems that Zara did most of the running. Richard was slightly surprised to find himself being drawn closer to the Queen's granddaughter.

They must have had a great deal in common; both lived for horses and all their friends were involved in the sport in one way or another. One of the first things that attracted Richard to Zara was her complete lack of pretension or arrogance. But he wasn't too surprised, as her mother had shown the same qualities. Zara joined in the friendly banter of the stables and always gave as good as she got. In everyday life, as on horseback, she was certainly no shrinking violet.

At first, theirs was a clandestine affair, conducted behind the closed doors of 'safe' houses provided by friends of the couple who could be relied upon to be discreet. It all added piquancy to the relationship and gave it a certain frisson of excitement. It was fairly easy for them to meet whenever Richard's diary allowed. Zara was free most of the time and she fitted in with his timetable. They took things slowly, eating leisurely lunches and dinners when he had a free day, which wasn't all that often, and they usually made up a party with friends so that no one could point a finger and say they were a couple. It was months before the press got an inkling of them being together and it was because of this that they were able to get to know each other well before they committed themselves.

As the relationship developed, Richard took Zara home to meet his parents at the family farm in Herefordshire, where his mother breeds and trains horses on their land. His father and mother, Keith and Sue Johnson, made her welcome, as did his brother, Nick, who runs the family farm, but they didn't treat her any differently from any of the other friends Richard had brought home.

The Johnson family are steeped in racing; Richard's father was a successful amateur jockey and rode in the Grand National, and with a grandfather on his mother's side holding a training licence, all of them, with the exception of Nick, are passionate about the sport. Another interest that drew Richard and Zara together was their love of hunting. Both families enjoyed the thrill of hunting, until legislation put a stop to it. Richard and Zara enjoyed simple pleasures, such as long country walks and pub lunches at rural inns, which they loved to discover in the villages near where they lived. It was all far removed from the glamorous Royal weekends at Windsor Castle and Christmas parties at Sandringham with the Queen, Prince Philip and, back in those days, Queen Elizabeth, the Queen Mother, who, as a life-long aficionado of racing 'over the sticks', thoroughly approved of Zara's friendship with one of the country's most acclaimed National Hunt jockeys.

Friends of the Princess Royal, who know Zara both as a member of the Royal Family and as an equestrian, say she is like a chameleon, in that she can adapt to changing circumstances apparently without effort, changing from a Royal one day to a pub-going local girl the next. It's all the same to her. But Richard was hardly a local working-class boy made good. He had been educated at boarding school, after the Cathedral Prep School in Hereford, and passed his exams. His family are country people with substantial farming interests and no shortage of money, and are well respected in the county where they live. With the education they paid for, Richard could have gone in for almost any profession he chose. Racing was his aim right from the start.

Richard and Zara were determined not to rush things and they took their time before they decided to move in together. Richard already had a house of his own, an elegant, white-washed detached residence, not too far from Gatcombe, and Zara began staying overnight. Eventually they agreed it would make good sense to live together and she moved in with him.

One of the first times Zara and Richard went out on a date in London was to see the revival of the musical *The King and I*, which was being produced by James Erskine, a man for whom she had worked briefly in Sydney, and who is now her agent. Richard had been riding in Ireland during the day, so Zara went on ahead with her brother, and he followed later –

much later, as it happened. He was too late to see the show, which was ending by the time he arrived. Richard waited in an upstairs lounge for Zara to leave and they walked out of the theatre together, which was when he first discovered what it was like to be the partner of a member of the Royal Family. The press pack was out in force and dozens of them were jostling to get the best picture. When Zara emerged with Richard, the press went wild, snapping away, flashbulbs going off; it was utter chaos. Zara knew how to handle it – Royalty gets used to this sort of attention from an early age – but for Richard it was a baptism of fire, and he found it an unnerving experience.

As their relationship grew more serious, Zara began to follow Richard's career at racecourses around the country, where, of course, she was recognised wherever she went. Zara had started her career as a three day eventer by this stage, and Richard returned the compliment and accompanied her up and down the land. The only difference was that generally he could go around totally unrecognised. Their riding disciplines were so different that people who followed eventing rarely knew who Richard Johnson was. He was not, in those early days, a nationally recognisable figure.

When Richard and Zara were together, he encouraged her to take her sport seriously and concentrate on honing her skills. She already had the talent and even before she and Richard knew each other, she had horses in training. But she was still only a schoolgirl, with all the usual temptations that teenagers go through. By the time she and Richard settled down, Zara had finished studying at university and they both had riding careers to concentrate on, which meant they would often be at opposite ends of the country for days at a time. It didn't make for an ideal existence. As one of the most sought-after jockeys in the country, Richard would be booked up for months ahead, and often found himself flying from one racecourse to another on the same day. The National Hunt season has become a year-round affair, with racing taking place on up to 300 days a year. Sometimes when he got home, he found that Zara was competing at an event miles away and she was going to sleep in the horsebox overnight. The bills for their mobile phones were astronomical.

With Richard sometimes having seven rides a day, by the time he got home he was often exhausted, so the couple usually ended up sitting quietly in front of the television eating a take-away. Zara is a good cook and she loves to prepare extravagant meals when she gets the chance. But not knowing what time Richard was going to arrive home often meant cooking was a complete waste of time, so she didn't bother.

Considering they were both young, gregarious people, it comes as a surprise to learn that they preferred the quiet life in the country to the bright lights of London. Not that they didn't enjoy the occasional night out in the city, but their circle of friends came from the area where they lived and most of the time they all seemed to prefer a couple of hours in a local pub or restaurant. Zara openly admits that during the period she was with Richard Johnson she enjoyed drinking, perhaps more than she should have. But she never smoked or tried drugs. She also denied that she was once seen sprawling in the gutter, too drunk to know what was going on. In fact, she claims her favourite drink is a glass or two of red wine – or a nice cup of tea.

During the time they were together, Richard was able to mix easily with Zara's parents and her grandparents. There were no uncomfortable moments. He was accepted by the Queen and Prince Philip, who shared his love of horses, so they always had plenty to talk about. If he ever gave Her Majesty any racing tips, neither revealed the fact. But, as the Queen never bets anyway, the question is purely academic. The only time she has a wager is to buy a ticket in the annual sweepstake that is held in the Royal Box on Derby Day. The winnings only ever amount to £20 or £30, but she has won several times.

A significant fact following the break-up between Zara and Richard is that he is still on friendly terms with the Princess Royal and also with the Queen, who he sees from time to time, giving them an opportunity to chat about their mutual passion.

It is true that Zara's relationship with Johnson was volatile. They are both people who know their own minds, and constantly being in the public eye when they were together put a tremendous strain on them. They couldn't be on their best behaviour all the time, but there was clearly fault on both sides. Someone who worked at one of the pubs they frequented said the staff never knew what the couple was going to do next. The atmosphere between them could change in a second and the staff often saw Zara get up and walk out, obviously in a flaming temper over something Richard had said or done. And they never bothered to keep their voices down when they were arguing, so everybody in the bar witnessed the quarrels. Most of them thoroughly enjoyed these spectacles, saying Zara and Richard provided free cabaret.

Zara has denied there were public rows, claiming they had a relaxed and calm relationship. Well, whatever the true facts, they did stay together for three years, so there must have been something rather special between them to keep them living together for so long. Zara could have gone home to Mum at any time if she had wanted to.

Towards the end of their relationship, Richard turned up very late at Zara's elegant 21st birthday party, given for her by the Queen at Windsor Castle. His excuse was that he had been riding at an evening meeting, which was confirmed, and as a professional, he could not let the trainer down. Zara knew about his programme, but she wasn't too pleased at being left alone for a large part of the evening.

One of the advantages of being the Queen's granddaughter, even if the Princess Royal insists her children are not Royal themselves, is that they are allowed, indeed, expected to avail themselves of some of the privileges of Royalty. Zara's 21st was just such an occasion. Everything was paid for by Her Majesty and it was considered to be the highlight of the year. The party took place in the vaulted undercroft of the castle, in what used to be the servants' hall, transformed for the occasion into a fairytale grotto. Hundreds of Moroccan lanterns provided the illumination and the whole room was decorated in blue and silver by Bentley Entertainments, the party organiser company run by Peregrine Armstrong-Jones, the half-brother of Lord Snowdon, the Queen's former brother-in-law. Mr Armstrong-Jones is arguably Britain's leading Society party planner, having organised the wedding of David and Victoria Beckham and also the fortieth birthday bash of the Princess Royal at Gatcombe Park in 1990.

Two hundred guests, including the Queen, Prince William and Prince Harry, filled the undercroft and danced to the party band Love Train, who played many of the hits of the 70s, including one of Zara's favourites, Diana Ross's 'Chain Reaction'. When Richard did arrive, Zara spent the evening in his arms, and at one point everyone was on the floor. Zara's Godfather, Andrew Parker Bowles, was present and had the honour of being seated next to the Queen at dinner, though the noise was so deafening that neither could hear what the other was saying.

The champagne flowed non-stop and the last guest did not depart until the early hours. Fortunately for Zara and Richard, they were staying at the castle so they didn't have to worry about drinking and driving. All the hotels and boarding houses within walking distance of the castle had been booked up months in advance, so no one had too far to go. The next morning there were several hangovers, but everyone agreed it had been a night to remember.

When Zara and Richard eventually broke up, it was a mutual decision. No one else was involved. Zara didn't meet Mike Tindall in Australia until after the parting with Johnson. They both believed the affair had simply run out of steam. Richard's lateness to Zara's party may have been irritating, but it wasn't the main contributing factor to the break-up. They had already decided to go their own ways, as each was progressing up the ladder in their separate sports; in Richard's case, it was his job. They were seeing less and less of each other, spending little time in Richard's house, so Zara moved out.

They have remained on good terms since the parting, and occasionally meet at social functions. And if Zara does marry Mike Tindall, Richard's name will surely be included on the guest list. Several of Zara's friends were secretly pleased that the relationship had broken down because they thought that Zara's feelings for Richard blinded her to her own ambitions and distracted her from her riding. It was only when the relationship began to cool that the full strength of Zara's ambition as a rider manifested itself. Before that, she was content to bask in the reflected glory of her boyfriend's success. Now it was her turn to aim for the top.

7 LOVE LIFE (PART TWO)

It would be difficult to imagine Zara with anyone but a sportsman for a boyfriend. She lives and breathes sport and the idea of her with someone who doesn't just isn't on. So few were surprised when she teamed up with a giant rugby player from Yorkshire, even though Mike Tindall, who was born on 18 October 1978 in Wakefield and educated at Queen Elizabeth Grammar School, Northgate, could scarcely be said to come from the same side of the tracks as Zara. But then, who could make that claim? She is, after all, eleventh in line to the throne, with open access to Buckingham Palace and Windsor Castle, and numbers Prince Andrew, Duke of York, among her Godparents, even if she does not have a title of her own – apart from World Champion of course! But, as with the mutual attraction of her parents, Zara was looking for someone who had excelled at his sport. This was what happened when Princess Anne first met Mark Phillips. At that time, he was the better rider, and that was what made him attractive in her eyes. In equestrian terms, they were both pure thoroughbreds, if not exactly out of the same stable.

It was in November 2003 during the Rugby World Cup in Australia that Zara and Mike first met. Her family's love of rugby has been well documented. Anne is Patron of the Scottish Rugby Union, and the national team's most ardent supporter, while Zara's brother, Peter, won a cap playing for Scotland Schools. He and Zara were in Australia to watch England and it was at a party celebrating England's victory in the semi-final that Mike Tindall was first introduced to the Queen's granddaughter. He hadn't played in the match and wasn't feeling at his best, but meeting her gave him a lift, and they hit it off from the word go. The star of that evening's celebrations was Zara's cousin, Prince Harry, arguably the Royal Family's most enthusiastic party-goer, and it was he who brought them together.

Tindall was selected to play in the final on 22 November in Sydney, which, history has recorded, England won, with Jonny Wilkinson's superb drop goal in the last minutes of the game. Later that evening, Prince Harry texted one of the players to see if he could join them at the after-match party, and he brought Peter and Zara along with him. Mike Tindall recalls that that evening was when he and Zara first got to know each other and swapped mobile telephone numbers.

But there were rumours that while she was in Australia, Zara had enjoyed a short romantic interlude with another rugby player, Caleb Ralph, the New Zealand All Black wing three-quarter. They had met after the All Blacks had played France and, according to press reports, which were not denied, they spent three days in each other's company. There was so much speculation about the couple that in January 2004 Ralph called a press conference in New Zealand to put the matter straight. He admitted that he had travelled to England to spend Christmas and New Year with Zara. He said, 'I have been in England and I did see her.' But he declined to go into details about their relationship, saying, 'I don't want to discuss that. I really think that is private, and it's my private life.'

According to newspaper reports, the pair had spent Christmas together and later joined Mark Phillips at Aston Farm to celebrate the New Year. On New Year's Day they went together to the Cheltenham Races but refused to answer any questions about their relationship. Ralph then returned to

New Zealand and at his press conference was unable to confirm that Zara was going to join him, or that she might be staying with him. 'I don't know,' he said. 'I'd just have to wait and see.' If there was a romance, it didn't last long, and petered out shortly after Mike Tindall appeared on the scene.

When the England team returned home in triumph from Australia, Zara and Mike were first photographed together outside the Met Bar in London and she later invited him to Gatcombe to meet her parents. This was early in 2004. They give different versions of how the invitation came about. Mike reckons she just asked him. She says he bombarded her with text messages until she gave in. Whatever the truth, that first visit to Gatcombe proved to be a great success. Mike got on famously with the Princess Royal and her ex-husband, though he later said he was nervous at first, but that they soon put him at ease. Again it was a case of both Anne and Mark liking the company of people who have done well at sports. This was the case when Anne first met Richard Meade, Andrew Parker Bowles and, later, Jackie Stewart. Zara recalls that first meeting with her parents as something of a nightmare for Mike, a description he says is very much an exaggeration.

After Mike met her parents, Zara decided she wanted to take things a little further and phoned Mike to invite him to accompany her to the North Cotswold Hunt Ball at Sudeley Castle. He recalled, 'She asked me if I fancied going to the ball and I replied that I had never been to one and I'd give it a crack.' So they went together and had a really good time, but Mike later said it occurred to him that it would give him something to chat to the Queen about when he and the England team joined her for tea at Buckingham Palace. For Mike it was the second time he had been paired up with a celebrity. The first was when he went on a blind date with the socialite Tara Palmer-Tompkinson, organised by a magazine as a publicity stunt. That occasion was not repeated.

Zara and Mike both agree though that their relationship is based on good friendship. Mike has said, 'We are the best of mates,' while Zara says, 'We share the same ridiculous sense of humour.'

In October 2004, Mike and the rest of the victorious England team were again invited to Buckingham Palace, where they were presented with MBEs by the Queen. In the audience, along with the other wives and girlfriends, was Zara, who was obviously delighted to see her man honoured by her grandmother. Later they held hands as they attend a celebratory lunch party.

Mike (or to give him his full name, Michael James) Tindall, MBE, with his simple Yorkshire roots and down-to-earth in-built charm, isn't overawed by being in the presence of the Royal Family. He has met the Queen and other members of the family on many social occasions since being with Zara, and he hasn't let any of it go to his head. His very naturalness is the secret of his attraction. He is still the same Wakefield lad he was when he lived there, and no matter how close he has become to Royalty, he had never once tried to be anything but what he is.

Of course, his own sporting achievements speak for themselves. Apart from being a member of that now-legendary England side, he negotiated a lucrative contract when he moved from Bath to Gloucester, his present club, in 2005. The move is also very convenient for his and Zara's domestic arrangements, the club being just half-an-hour's drive from Gatcombe. It was following the 1999 Rugby World Cup, when both Jeremy Guscott and Phil de Glanville retired that Mike became a regular in the national side at inside centre, winning 41 caps. In the last two years he has suffered injuries to his shoulder and foot that have kept him out of contention, but he is now back in full training, and has regained the form he needed to get back into the England squad and make the starting line-up wearing the number thirteen jersey.

Zara was delighted when Mike regained his place in the England team, which he did with gusto in February 2007, playing at Twickenham in a record-breaking victory over Scotland. It was a red-letter day, as Mike was celebrating his fiftieth cap for his country, and Zara was there to cheer him on. Now they are both at the top of the tree in their respective sports. If he was frustrated by not being in the national side for three years through injury and loss of form, he gave little outward sign. His colleagues at Gloucester say he is one of the easiest guys to get along with – off the field. On it, he is a tiger: fearless, fast and incisive. Given his size, Mike Tindall is a formidable opponent and one of the Scottish side said being tackled by him was like running into a brick wall.

Zara was in the crowd again at Twickenham in March when Mike scored the winning try against France, and she yelled herself hoarse. She has now become the unofficial mascot of the England team and never misses a game. A knee injury sustained when scoring that winning try meant Mike had to sit out the final match against Wales at the Millennium Stadium in Cardiff. England duly lost the game.

Mike has been credited with being a great help to Zara when she was preparing for her attempt at the World Championship in Aachen. The Great Britain Olympic equestrian team manager, Yogi Breisner, says, 'Being with Mike really helps Zara because he is a dedicated sportsman. They inspire each other.'

Mike's colleagues at Gloucester Rugby Club say she has been just as much help to him. It's of mutual benefit, because neither feels the need to go out drinking every night at the local pub. They are both too fitness conscious, so they prefer to spend their evenings quietly at home. Not that they do not enjoy themselves. They certainly are young people of their time, and when the occasion demands, they can party with the best of them. But during the working week, it's early to bed and early to rise.

Zara likes to give occasional dinner parties at their home on the Gatcombe Estate. These are fairly small, intimate affairs and they limit the number of guests to around six or eight, as they find this is a number that enables everyone to enjoy conversation around the table. An evening with the couple is lively and relaxed, and while the talk may be mainly about sport, as their guests are usually people of their own age who are involved in either rugby or equitation, or both, they also know a number of people from showbusiness and they love to hear the latest gossip from the world of theatre, film and television. There is only one topic that is taboo and that is, naturally enough, the Royal Family. Zara never discusses any member of the family and if a guest happens to mention her grandmother, Zara always refers to her as the Queen or Her Majesty, never Granny. Dinner with Zara and Mike is usually an informal meal, but on special occasions they might stipulate black tie, as Zara does like dressing up now and then. If someone is invited to stay for the weekend and asks for the dress code, they are usually told, 'Just a pair of jeans and a dinner jacket.' It's that sort of household. Zara is a brilliant hostess and goes to endless trouble to make sure her guests have everything they need. If she requires any help from the big house, there are always plenty of willing hands available to help prepare a meal or serve drinks. It does help to have the Princess Royal as a mother on these occasions.

Zara's friends make up a close-knit circle and she doesn't care if they are well known or not. If they get on, that's good enough for her, just as long as they are loyal and unpretentious, two of the qualities she admires more than any others. The rules governing friendship with a member of the Royal Family, even one without a title, are complex and, to outsiders, sometimes impossible to understand. With the older Royals, such as the Queen and Prince Philip, there is never the slightest risk of overstepping the mark, but with some of the younger members it is easy to confuse friendliness with familiarity.

Together Zara and Mike make an attractive couple: he, with his commanding height; she, at just 5ft 5ins. When he says she looks up to him, she replies, 'Oh! Yeah?' He is a much calmer person than Zara. She is liable to fly off the handle if things go wrong, particularly in the run-up to a major competition, when something, or someone, in the stables has upset her. She doesn't sulk, but, like her mother, she does not watch her tongue. She simply lets rip with the sort of ripe language that is prevalent in equestrian circles. Mike has a calming influence on Zara. He is able to soothe her feelings when others look for cover. Everybody who knows them says it is since they began living together that Zara has settled down. She no longer has time, or the inclination, to drop in to her local pub, the Ragged Cot Inn, as she used to when she was with Richard Johnson. In those days she was a regular, both at lunchtimes and in the evening. She was extremely popular with the local crowd and she was never alone, always accompanied by groups of friends, or occasionally her father. These days alcohol is strictly limited and as she rides up to eight hours a day, week in, week out, fitness is a number one priority, with her diet equally strictly controlled so there isn't much chance of her putting on extra pounds. Being happy and content with Mike seems to have transformed Zara's life. She has reached the very top of her sport, and she has every intention of staying there.

There is a certain amount of good-natured banter in the Gloucester dressing-room about the fact that Mike is squiring a member of the Royal Family, but it's no more than friendly ribbing, of the kind that every sportsman with a celebrity girlfriend experiences. Mike and Zara are not quite in the Beckham celebrity class – which suits them both very well – but in their own circle, there's no doubt that he has gone up in his team-mates' eyes through his association with Zara Phillips, champion of the world and granddaughter of the monarch.

They both compete in dangerous sports, but Mike says you cannot really compare the two. 'You get a lot of minor injuries in rugby and sometimes big collisions, but you make a mistake and something goes wrong in eventing and the reality is if a horse falls on you, it's potentially fatal.' He adds, 'Zara's so skilful, I'm fully confident in her ability. She knows exactly what to do.'

A little-known fact about Mike Tindall is that he is a poker fanatic. His love for the game began when he started playing on his computer during his enforced rest after his rugby injuries. He was hooked straightaway, and in the summer of 2006 was invited to take part in a televised 'All Star Poker Challenge' by ITV. He accepted because the prize money was going to a charity of the winner's choice. In his case, he nominated the Parkinson's Disease Society, because his father suffers from the illness.

In the final of the competition, Mike found he was playing against the Welsh former World Snooker Champion, Mark Williams, another poker fanatic. Eventually, Mike ran out the winner, in a Texas Hold 'Em showdown, with his pair of jacks beating Williams' pair of fives. Mike's chosen charity benefited to the tune of £25,000. After his win, Mike said he had an ambition to one day visit Las Vegas and play in the World Series of Poker. Zara's reaction to this has not yet been revealed, but she did hang around patiently for eight hours in Cardiff when he was playing in the final.

If it is true that opposites attract, then Zara and Mike are perfect examples. He is the calm, methodical type who doesn't get upset or irritated by many things; Zara is the more volatile member of the partnership. She sometimes speaks without thinking and she wears her heart on her sleeve. They are a very tactile couple, usually seen holding hands when they are together, and they do not mind being seen kissing in public. Zara is very affectionate and obviously adores Mike, feelings he returns in full, if not quite so openly.

One of the nicest things about their relationship is the obvious pleasure each takes in the other's success. Mike is extremely proud of Zara's victories on horseback, while she supports him at every opportunity when he is playing for Gloucester. She loves to sit in the stands watching the matches with some of the other wives and girlfriends, but unlike the WAGs of some of the top celebrity soccer players, she does not enjoy the never-ending round of parties and premieres that seem to be the staple diet of these young ladies. Neither does she fling her money around, buying the latest 'must-have' jewellery and designer handbags. Her favourite clothes are jeans, the older the better, and she owns a wide selection of chunky sweaters. Sometimes she looks as if she has just thrown on the first thing that has come to hand, which may be true, but when the occasion demands she looks like a million dollars. Mike also has the build to show off clothes to their best advantage, but he too prefers the casual look around the house.

It could be daunting for someone in his position and with his background to have to socialise with the Queen and the Duke of Edinburgh if he were not so confident of his ability to mix with people from all walks of life and every class. But Mike gets on well with the Royal Family and enjoys a good argument with Prince Philip when they meet to chat about rugby. Of course, Philip loves to provoke arguments, and he goes to extraordinary lengths to contradict someone else's opinions, even if, privately, he agrees with them, just to get them arguing. Mike quickly found out that the way to enjoy the company of Zara's grandfather was to take him on head-to-head and not give in. Prince Philip respected Mike's attitude and the Queen was quietly amused at the way her granddaughter's boyfriend stood up to her husband.

One result of Mike's relationship with Zara is that he has become involved with the equine world, not as a rider or competitor, but as a part-owner. He and former England prop, Jason Leonard, joined a syndicate that owns a racehorse named Cash Converter. Mike said it was a welcome distraction from the intense pressure of playing rugby, and the deep frustration of being injured.

Friends of Mike and Zara say he is a man of definite opinions on most subjects, but he is not dogmatic. He will listen to the other person's point of view, particularly if they are knowledgeable about the topic, but he rarely changes his mind once it is made up.

Zara learned from an early age that, as a member of the Royal Family, she has to be careful about what she says in public, knowing it could reflect badly on her grandmother. She says the main problem she has with the press is that if she tells them anything interesting, they never take any notice.

At home on the Gatcombe estate, Mike and Zara have settled down to what appears to be an idyllic domestic lifestyle. They live in one of the nicest parts of Britain, on a large estate, with all the advantages and none of the responsibilities. They have no money worries, can come and go as they please and their pleasures are simple to say the least. Zara loves watching the 'soaps' on television, with *EastEnders* being her current favourite. One of her other much-watched programmes are recordings of *My Family*, starring Robert Lindsay and Zoë Wannamaker. On her own admission, she is not an intellectual and books are not seen in abundance around the house. In fact, she admits that she hardly ever reads anything that isn't to do with horses.

At the time of writing, because of their sporting commitments, they have not had many opportunities to go away together on holiday. But there are plenty of 'safe' houses available, belonging to friends of the Princess Royal, should they want the odd weekend away without worrying too much about prying eyes. And they would both like the chance to go on a world cruise with a group of close pals. Realistically, they cannot see that happening in the near future. Perhaps they should ask Zara's uncle, the Prince of Wales, who knows plenty of people with luxury yachts and who would, no doubt, be only too delighted to put them at the disposal of his niece.

Before she settled down with Mike, Zara had only to be seen in the company of a man for their names to be romantically linked. She once chatted in a friendly fashion with a famous British Formula One racing driver at an event where her brother was working. Peter had arranged for her to go into the pits to see the cars up close and to meet some of the drivers. The next day stories appeared in the papers saying they were a couple. There was no truth in it, of course, but it made good headlines: the Queen's granddaughter and the glamorous racing driver. As far as anyone knows they have not met from that day to this, but newspaper archives will revive the story the next time either of them does something newsworthy. And it's happened many times with Zara. To be fair, she hasn't always discouraged reporters from writing about her love life and after the Richard Johnson affair, conducted with all the discretion of a Hollywood press release, the press couldn't be blamed for assuming she couldn't be without a man in her life.

To Zara, breaking the rules of accepted conventional behaviour is second nature. But despite this, the 'Royal Rebel' tag, which she hates, and which was actually a tabloid invention when they ran stories about her body piercing, revealing necklines and her involvement with the occasional Antipodean, is a misnomer because, when the occasion demands, she can be as haughty and conventional as any of her Royal relatives. Prince Charles has been called a 'Royal Rebel' because of his alleged meddling in political matters, and Princess Anne, when she was younger, was often described in the same way when reporters saw her driving at high speed around London in her Reliant sports car, with its distinctive personal number plate: 1420H (it represented one of her regiments). Anne was rarely seen with any of the 'right' type of young man in tow when she visited the fashionable nightspots of the time. Instead of the chinless wonders who graced the usual Royal circles in those days, she would often be in the company of someone she had met out hunting or on a sports field. She followed her instincts with aggressive openness – even when it came to the two men she married, neither of whom came from families that would have been considered suitable to provide escorts for the daughter of the sovereign. In that way, Zara is very much like her mother. She too breaks the rules, but because she is attractive and has an engaging personality, a modern outlook and, of course, because of her sporting success, she has endeared herself to an entire generation of young women – if not to their parents.

Zara has never tried to hide the fact that she likes men. She has been dating since she was in her early teens and has enjoyed friendships with young men, mostly sportsmen, from both hemispheres. As long as they shared her passion for all things athletic, they were OK with her. Now though, Mike is the only one. He is even taking lessons so he can take part in the Gatcombe weekend shooting parties with the 12-bore shotgun Zara bought him. Next he'll be buying a pair of jodhpurs and learning to ride.

A friend of Zara's says she is always smiling when Mike is around and they never seem to row. Perhaps it's his size that makes him so patient and confident. He knows he doesn't have to try to impress Zara and with both of them being members of World Cup winning teams, they have reached the top of their professions well before their thirtieth birthdays. Love is not a word they bandy around lightly. But if they are not in love, whatever they have got they should bottle and sell. Then they would both be multi-millionaires.

Because Mike and Zara have been living together for nearly two years and theirs is an exclusive relationship, there has obviously been speculation that they will marry in the near future. If it does happen, they will have to consider the timing with great care. When a member of the Royal Family marries, forward planning is taken to extreme lengths. All sorts of things have to be considered: the diary of the Queen is number one, and Her Majesty's engagements are usually arranged up to two years in advance, so if Zara and Mike were to become engaged – and Royal engagements rarely last more than six months – the date of the wedding would have to be announced practically on the same day. Then if a more senior member of the family wanted to marry – Prince William perhaps (although his much-publicised break-up with his girlfriend, Kate Middleton, seems to have put that possibility on hold)? – his preference for a date would take precedence. Prince William's wedding would obviously be a State occasion at Westminster Abbey or St Paul's Cathedral, which would take months of planning. Zara's would probably be in St George's Chapel at Windsor Castle, a smaller, but equally 'Royal' affair.

But do the couple want to marry? Zara laughs – with embarrassment – when the question is put to her and says, 'Do you see a ring?' But their closest friends say they are in love and believe they will marry, maybe once the Olympic Games and the Rugby World Cup are over. We'll have to wait and see.

If there were something that would really seal their happiness it would be for Zara to add an Olympic gold medal to her World title, and for England to win the next World Cup, with Mike scoring the winning try. And who knows? Both could happen.

8 A FROCK FOR ALL SEASONS

Raunchy, outrageous, adventurous, trendy, shocking, casual and chic, smart and sexy: those are just some of the words that have been used to describe Zara's dress sense in the past. Socks sporting pictures of Homer Simpson, stockings bearing Union Jack flags worn under a revealing mini-skirt at Christmas with the Queen, an 'inside-out' sheepskin coat with fur stripes, and a £1,000 maroon patchwork leather-and-cashmere coat by Mulberry. They are all part of Zara's expanding wardrobe and are sure to get her picture in the papers and fashion magazines.

One of the guaranteed measures of whether a celebrity has 'arrived' is whether newspapers and magazines publish stories about their clothes. In Zara's case, her outfits attracted so much comment at the 2007 Cheltenham Festival that bookmakers started taking bets on what she would be wearing. Irish bookmaker Paddy Power accepted many bets and is said to have paid out £10,000 to punters who forecast that Zara would wear brown shoes on Gold Cup day. It was a clear sign that Zara was ahead in the style stakes.

Zara has always loved clothes, but she is less fond of shopping, so visits to the West End showrooms of fashionable designers are rare. Instead she relies on a friend who runs a dress shop in Broadway, near her home, and who is able to supply nearly everything that she wears. If the shop hasn't got it in stock, the friend will obtain it within days.

In her teens, Zara's standard garb was jeans and T-shirts, with the obligatory waxed Barbour jacket and green Hunter boots at horse trials or around the estate at home. She still prefers the casual look, but now accepts that, as a public figure, she has an image to live up to, so she dresses accordingly. She knows that when she attends a film premiere on the arm of Mike Tindall, glamorous clothes are essential, even though the outfits worn by celebrities on such occasions are more often borrowed than bought. The elaborate confections yield all the publicity the designers could ask for as the flashbulbs pop.

According to a source at Mulberry, 'She's the transitional face of the Royals and she's very beautiful.' Zara is one of those fortunate women who look good whatever they wear. One British designer said that she could literally wear a sack and still look fantastic. Not that there's much chance of Zara trying to prove those words right. She loves clothes and she knows she looks her best when she is dressed up to the nines.

Around the yard at home when she is working with her horses, she is strictly a jeans-and-sweater type, saying you can't muck out stables in high-heeled Jimmy Choos and a silk dress. But when the occasion demands, she is up there with the leading fashion icons of the day. Sleek, tailored trousersuits and dresses in silk and cashmere are shown to their best advantage over her fabulous size ten figure.

Zara is aware that when she appears in public, every detail is going to be put under public and media scrutiny, and while, in previous years, she was prepared to go out in hipster jeans showing an expanse of belly between her waistband and top, those days have long gone.

When she goes to the races, the other race-goers all watch to see what she will be wearing on each day, and they are never disappointed. As much attention goes into selecting every outfit as into trying to pick a winner. In the Royal style stakes, Zara is clearly ahead of the field, having almost taken over from the late Diana, Princess of Wales, as a one-woman fashion industry. Young women of her own age group see her as an icon, particularly if they are interested in the equestrian scene. Zara doesn't care for the description herself, thinking it makes her out to be nothing but a walking clotheshorse, and she feels it detracts from the more serious side of her career as a world-class horsewoman.

But as she has got older, she has realised that because of her position within the Royal Family, it is important for her to maintain a sense of dignity when she is on show, so she dresses accordingly, though she did once shock fellow members in the Royal Enclosure at Ascot when she appeared wearing a dress split to the hip. Previously she had also been seen in a scarlet dress that left nothing to the imagination on top. You could see just about everything she had to show without getting arrested.

Zara does not follow the latest fashions slavishly and says she only dresses for the job, meaning when she is going out in public and she knows there is more than a possibility of being photographed. She does have an innate sense of style and has the ability to choose those clothes that are right for her. The demands of her position as the Queen's granddaughter mean she cannot wear the same outfit twice if she attends a film or theatre premiere; that would quickly be commented upon by the newspapers. As a result Zara needs a substantial wardrobe, because on these public occasions she is seen to be a representative of the Royal Family, even when she is attending in a private capacity. In recent years, just about every public appearance has been followed by photographs showing every detail of her outfit.

Ever since Princess Diana, there has been a public fixation with Royal fashion that has focussed attention on British designers to an extent never before experienced. Royalty has rarely patronised more than one or two dress designers. The Queen and Queen Mother used Norman Hartnell and Hardy Amies exclusively for years before they decided to include other couturiers.

Unlike Zara and Diana, none of the other women in the Royal Family is considered to be particularly stylish in the accepted sense of the word. They generally regard the need to choose their clothes carefully as being a necessary but troublesome aspect of being Royal. Their outfits are chosen for three reasons: they must be suitable for the job, they must be functional, and they should be comfortable, as they may have to be worn for hours at a time in varying conditions. The Queen's style has barely changed since she came to the throne in 1952; the Queen Mother retained her own unique style throughout her life: acres of floating chiffon that would look ridiculous on anyone else, but they suited her, and that was all she cared about. The Princess Royal is happiest in a waxed jacket and Wellington boots, but accepts that she must make an effort when she is 'on duty'. The Duchess of Cornwall knows what she likes and sticks to it, even if her style has been described as 'frumpy' (although her dress sense has improved since she married into the family), while the Duchess of York, although not technically still a Royal, has a dress sense that is said to be a contradiction in terms. One of the more peculiar things about Fergie is the way in which she dresses her daughters, Beatrice and Eugenie, in near-matching outfits that have nothing to do with their looks, figures or age. When mother and daughters appeared together on one occasion they looked like caricatures of the Beverley Sisters.

It was Diana who revolutionised British fashion and the perception of the Royal Family practically single-handedly, and certainly it was she who revived the millinery industry almost overnight. Zara has inherited her love of *haute couture* from Diana, not from her own mother, who, while invariably appearing smart, could never be described as fashion-conscious. Though in her youth the Princess was seen in fashionable mid-thigh length mini-skirts, as soon as she began to play an active part in the Royal Family's public duties, she was restricted by the regal formality that distinguishes all that the senior ladies wear.

The thought of the Queen in her youth wearing a dress that

ended some way above the knee would have given the Royal Household the vapours. In recent years, Her Majesty has become more daring in her choice of clothes. Designers such as the late Ian Thomas and Maureen Rose persuaded her that there was no reason why she should not appear more contemporary without losing any of her personal dignity and charisma. You could say that instead of the Queen catching up with fashion, fashion has caught up with her, as the 'lady-like' look now seems to be coming back. The latest person to help Her Majesty with her wardrobe is her senior dresser and personal assistant Angela Kelly. Miss Kelly, a former sergeant in the army, now designs many of her mistress's outfits herself and they are made up or altered in a workroom in Buckingham Palace. Angela's influence is enormous, and she is credited with improving the Queen's appearance almost single-handedly, without the aid of any of the high-priced professional designers who have traditionally worked for Her Majesty for many years.

As a younger member of the Royal Family, Zara is not yet constrained by the rules governing the rest of the ladies in the family; she can buy what she likes and, within reason, wear what she wants. And because of the lack of real style amongst the other Royal ladies, with the possible exception of Lady Helen Taylor, daughter of the Duke of Kent, she is regarded by many as the glamour girl of the Windsors. Zara is clearly relishing her current position as the leading and most stylish Royal. It certainly doesn't do her image any harm, and her sponsors are delighted that their newest 'face' is constantly in the public eye, looking good.

Zara docs not often buy off-the-peg clothes. She patronises some of the new, innovative young British designers such as Ashley Isham, who created a stunning grey silk coat and dress for her to wear at Royal Ascot in 2006. It was an outstanding success.

Zara doesn't always rely on her own taste when she is looking for new clothes and she has, in the past, even hired a celebrity stylist, Ceril Campbell, who is said to charge up to

£500 a day, to give her advice on what to wear and where to buy it. It was due to Ceril's influence that Zara has been seen in outfits by designers such as Vivienne Westwood (at her 21st birthday party she wore a Westwood creation that combined a corset with a slit skirt that opened as she walked and was delicately described as 'extremely figure hugging'), Betty Jackson, Amanda Wakely, Moschino and Dolce et Gabbana. But she does know what she wants to look like and will argue with her stylist and designers if they suggest something she thinks will look ridiculous on her. As the client, she knows she has the final word and, as she is paying large sums for some of her outfits, she demands value for money.

Ceril and Zara work as a team when selecting outfits. Ceril says she likes Zara's clothes to be understated so that they can provide a perfect background for Zara's natural beauty. That is why they chose the soft colours of lilac and silver for Ascot.

One of the problems in dressing Zara is that she sometimes will not make up her mind until the last minute. There was one race meeting when Zara gave her dress designer, Elspeth Gibson, just 48 hours' notice to come up with the outfit she wanted. Elspeth worked non-stop and, of course, the dress was ready on the day.

One great advantage Zara has found in having Ceril's expertise at her disposal is that the professional stylist is able to stand back and visualise the whole picture. While Zara knows what she wants in dresses and suits, it can be difficult to imagine what sort of shoes, hat and handbag are needed to complete the ensemble.

On at least one occasion, Ceril took Zara to meet milliner Tara O'Callaghan, who suggested what turned out to be the perfect hat for Ascot, and then Christian Louboutin provided the shoes to match, though they did have five-inch heels that were not all that practical for walking about in the Royal Enclosure. The next day Zara again wore high-heeled shoes and her hat was once more designed by Tara O'Callaghan. This time it was a trilby, with huge feathers and a bow. Zara was definitely making a statement. That was the year when a poll of British women placed Zara in the winning position as the celebrity who wore hats better than anyone else. Her aunt-by-marriage, the Duchess of Cornwall, came second, with Victoria Beckham third.

Zara had travelled from her home in Gloucestershire to Ascot wearing a casual striped top and white skirt on both days. She surprised some of the other ladies by popping into the lavatory and changing her clothes. When she emerged, she looked like a million dollars. Ceril had travelled to Ascot to be with Zara, and, unusually for a member of the Royal Family, Zara allowed her to talk to reporters about her outfits. Ceril said she had been aiming for the 'Audrey Hepburn' look for Zara, who was obviously happy with the Fifties style of her outfits. The designers chosen by Ceril and Zara were obviously also delighted at the publicity they were getting from their Royal client, which was just as well, as celebrities are rarely asked to pay the full retail price for the clothes they wear – as long as they mention the name of the designer. Many designers will either give or lend their clothes to someone famous to wear to a public event, or at least sell them at such a reduced price that they are cheaper than the average High Street department store. Jewellers also queue up to lend their priceless tiaras, necklaces and diamond bracelets, on the same commercial basis.

Zara and Ceril Campbell forged a strong partnership that favoured both parties. Ceril got her fees and wonderful publicity, while Zara appeared better dressed than she had ever been before. Everyone was happy.

With the current vogue for models with size zero figures, Zara is never going to be the darling of the commercial fashion world. She is too womanly, with an impressive bust, shapely hips and long, elegant but strong legs. Zara is not likely to be asked to stroll along any catwalk in Paris, New York or London, yet when she is seen wearing a mini-skirt above calf-length boots, all topped off with a flat-brimmed cap, she can easily be mistaken for an international fashion model. She has demonstrated that fashion does not have to be restricted to the catwalk and that special clothes can be worn for ordinary, everyday occasions, as long as they fit and flatter the wearer.

When Zara and Mike attend an evening engagement in London, there is an air of sophistication that heightens the sense of occasion. They both know they are on show: Mike looks good in evening dress with wide satin-faced lapels and black tie; Zara is stunning in whatever she chooses. Together they make an attractive pair – and they know it.

For years fashion houses have been associated with different celebrity events and sport has become the latest bandwagon on which the industry can hitch a ride. Burberry sponsors polo events, and you cannot get more upmarket than that; Ralph Lauren dressed every ball boy and umpire, and just about every other official, at Wimbledon last year, while Dunhill has done a deal to see its name on the sails and hulls of the yachts taking part in the Americas Cup in Valencia. What are the odds against one of the big names in fashion seizing the opportunity of being associated with the newest glamour sport, three day eventing? If one does come up with the money, no prizes for guessing which Royal world title holder will be high on their list of potential models – and it will make a nice change from the size zero frames usually seen in fashion magazines to see a woman who actually looks like a woman.

Of course, no one is likely to rush out and buy a dress or suit just because they have seen Zara wearing it, as they used to in the days when Diana led the world in fashion. Then, manufacturers fell over themselves to be the first to rush out copies of Diana's outfits. When she wore a Robin Hood-type hat, over a million copies were sold in Japan alone. That's not going to happen with Zara, but after she appeared with her cousins, William and Harry, outside Sandringham Parish Church on a Christmas morning, several of the crowd said afterwards that they thought she was a really good role model for younger women, both in her bearing and her dress sense. What Zara does possess is a feeling for what is right for her on different occasions, a sense of the right clothes for all seasons, and clothes for all reasons.

The Paris-based designer Roland Mouret has said, 'I think she is a fantastic woman. I love the light in her eyes. I'd love to dress her.' So would almost every other designer in Europe. The fact that she has a natural beauty and a figure that shows off clothes to their best advantage, combined with her celebrity status as Royal and a World Champion, makes her the sort of client any designer would die for.

Maureen Rose worked at designing dresses for the Queen for 30 years, first as assistant to Norman Hartnell, then with Ian Thomas and finally in her own right. She has known most of the ladies in the Royal Family and has opinions about what they all wear. I asked Mrs Rose what she thought of Zara's style. 'I think she is a one-off, and what she wears is excellent for a young person,' she said. 'She has the personality and figure to carry off outfits that would look ridiculous on other people, but on her they somehow look just right.

'What I like about Zara is that she is not afraid to try something new, even if it shocks. She is a bit raunchy and "with it", but very trendy, and I believe she sets a good example to young women today. However, when I have seen her with the Queen, she is as traditional as the rest of the family and I think her behaviour and manner is impeccable.'

Zara's fashion sense is not always universally applauded, however. At the wedding of the Prince of Wales and Camilla Parker Bowles, where the bride's outfit received widespread praise, Zara's Pucci shirt dress was less successful. One observer noted that it was more suitable for an afternoon's shopping trip than a Royal wedding. Of course, Royal weddings held in registry offices create great difficulties for the guests when they are deciding what to wear. Should they stick to safe, afternoon outfits and trouser suits or go the whole hog? Zara took the plunge with her Pucci frock, which showed an expanse of thigh and, as she wore it with several top buttons undone, a fair amount of cleavage. The vivid pattern shouted to be seen in teal, black and beige, and was worn with a black fedora trilby hat (*a la* Inspector Clouseau) and knee boots. It certainly made an impact on the fashion scene. Her mother didn't do too badly in the fashion stakes that day. Her bright royal blue fitted frock-coat with matching pill-box hat and veil suggested that she too had taken more than a little trouble with her outfit for the occasion.

David Emanuel is one of the world's leading dress designers. He has made clothes for Royalty, titled ladies, film stars such as Elizabeth Taylor and Joan Collins, pop stars like Madonna, and countless others in Society. Together with his then-wife, Elizabeth, David became a household name when he designed the most famous wedding dress in the world: the one that the late Diana, Princess of Wales, wore at her wedding in St Paul's Cathedral to the Prince of Wales in 1981. When I spoke to David about Zara Phillips and her style, he began by talking about her mother. 'The Princess Royal has the most fantastic figure and she wears the most ordinary clothes in an extraordinary way. She occasionally splashes out on something special and I was delighted to see her wearing an Emanuel dress in a beautiful gold colour when she was posed for a Norman Parkinson photograph in Buckingham Palace. I can think of no one who could have shown the dress off to better effect than Her Royal Highness.'

David thinks Zara adds sparkle to the younger generation of Royal ladies. 'She goes out to make a statement,' he says. 'I saw her at Royal Ascot wearing fabulous hats with huge feathers. At the same time, she is not a slave to fashion, so you couldn't call her a *fashionista*. She's on the fringe and wears what she likes, not what other people tell her to wear. In some ways, she is a "High Street" girl who gets it right nearly, but not quite, every time.'

David says that Royal ladies have never looked especially stylish, and that is how most people want them to look. At funerals and memorial services, Zara is seen in outfits just like the others: demure dresses that cover the knee, paired with hats and gloves. She cannot look too extreme because she is expected to resemble a Royal lady in the way that her mother did some 30 years ago.

When the occasion demands though, David Emanuel commented that she can look fabulous. 'The best thing I have seen her wear is a wrap-around cling dress in jersey. She has several in plain and pattern design and they are all exactly right for her. They make her look even more sexy than she is normally. She actually radiates sex appeal. She has emerged from the chrysalis and learned from her mistakes. The only other young Royal who rivals her is Lady Helen Taylor, who was the face of Armani for several years, and the sense of style still shows.'

Zara spends quite a lot of money on her clothes, but is able to offset some of the costs against expenses, as she usually is wearing the more expensive outfits on professional occasions, and like any other businessman or woman, she can claim them as legitimate outgoings. And, as with every other celebrity, she is often given dresses to wear by designers who want to be associated with her success – a sure sign that eventing has now become part of showbusiness.

David Emanuel says Zara knows she has to look her best because whenever she appears in public, she is going to be photographed. The pictures will find their way around the world, and she knows they need to reflect well on the Royal Family.

He adds, 'She has at last realised what suits her and what she looks good in after a few early mini-disasters. I'm sure there are pictures around now that she looks back on with horror. But then, so could all of us.' Talking about Zara's figure, David says, 'She has a fantastic body and she is in great shape from all those work-outs. It enables her to show off clothes to their best advantage and as a blonde she cannot fail with those lovely blues and greens she likes to wear.'

Inevitably, as Zara is living with Mike Tindall, there is speculation about their marriage plans. As David Emanuel designed 'that' dress back in 1981, how would he go about making a wedding dress for Zara?

'Everything moves on, including fashion and taste, so there is no way I could design a dress for Zara similar to the one I did for Lady Diana Spencer. In the first place, Diana was 5ft 10in and Zara is 5ft 5in, so you could not have something with a 25-foot train as Diana did. Then I would have to visit the venue with Zara. If the ceremony were to be in Westminster Abbey, it would be a very different wedding dress than if it were to be in the local village church. There is no one dress that would suit every occasion or venue. The dress has to suit the personality of the bride. I think Zara would be better with a cream dress than one of stark white. With Zara, as with all the brides I have designed for, I have to be involved with every aspect of the ensemble: dress, head covering, tiara, shoes, even stockings. I have seen women in the most elegant wedding dresses costing thousands of pounds and the whole effect ruined by a pair of shoes that looked like trainers. You also have to consider the flowers she would be carrying; that is very important as you don't want the dress to be obscured by a large bouquet. When I was dressing Diana, she came to see me carrying a selection of tiaras and asked me to choose one without telling me which was which. I chose one I thought was appropriate and by a happy coincidence she said it was the Spencer family tiara, so I got it right that time. I assume Zara will be offered a tiara by her mother or the Queen and I would like to be there when she decides. A Royal wedding is a wonderful occasion with the eyes of the world on the bride. Zara could be spectacular in Westminster Abbey but she would have to keep it simple if it is in the local church. Then I would advise her to hold back on the diamonds. She would be, I am sure, a beautiful bride and one of which the Royal Family would be justly proud.'

So what does he think could be Zara's future Royal role? 'She would be a wonderful ambassador for the Royal Family in the twenty-first century. She loves making a bold statement and she is young enough and beautiful enough to get away with it. She has the confidence that being a World Champion has given her, but she must be nurtured and brought on steadily so that we get the best out of her. There's been a huge void since Diana, Princess of Wales, died and Zara has emerged at just the right time. She is a real star in the making.'

9 A DAY IN THE LIFE OF . . .

The day always starts early in the Phillips/Tindall household. If it's a training day, the radio/alarm in the couple's comfortable bedroom goes off around 5.30 a.m. It must take a considerable amount of discipline on both their parts to rise at such an unearthly hour in order to make time for their training, day after day, summer and winter, no matter what the weather is like, but they accept that it is something they have to do if they are to remain at the top in their chosen careers.

Zara is usually the first one out of their king-size bed and she pads downstairs to make an early-morning cuppa for them both. Zara is a serious tea drinker. She cannot start the day without several cups of a strong brew, and when she and her grooms are working in the yard, the kettle is always on the boil. Visitors are asked if they would like tea; coffee is rarely offered. Zara likes only two drinks really: one is tea, the other is red wine. If she is out with friends in a local pub, the odd pint of beer might go down well, and for celebrations she might enjoy a glass or two of vintage champagne, unlike her mother, who never drinks any alcohol, even for official toasts. The Princess Royal usually sticks to soft drinks such as orange juice, mineral water or Coke, and when the Queen proposes a toast at a State Banquet, where the finest wines are drunk, she might raise her glass to her lips, but no one has ever seen her actually drink the champagne or drain the glass. Instead she swirls the wine around her glass to make it look as if she is enjoying it, but she barely wets her lips.

Zara and Mike are not the tidiest people in the world, on their own admission. They like comfort rather than luxury, but they do enjoy the services of a cleaner, who also works for the Princess Royal and Tim Laurence up at the big house. The laundry room does boast an industrial-size washing machine, which they need to cope with Zara's riding gear and the rugby shirts and sports outfits Mike wears whenever he is not on duty at Gloucester. The club launders everything he wears during a match, but Zara goes through several sets of riding clothes in a working week, so the washing machine seems never to be switched off.

The downstairs part of their home gives the impression that all is rather chaotic, with riding paraphernalia and rugby boots littering the floor and leaving one in no doubt that the occupants of this house are two sports-mad young people.

Breakfast is usually a fairly hurried and light affair. Neither eats a 'full English' during the week, though at weekends, when they are able to enjoy a more leisurely few days, they might treat themselves to the works.

As a professional rugby player, Mike is required to report for training every day, so he drives himself the twenty-odd miles to Gloucester in order to be there by 10 o'clock. He and Zara probably won't see each other until late that same evening, but they usually talk on their mobiles at some time during the day.

Zara has so many calls on her time that she not only has to train during the competition season, but also deal with correspondence (and thousands of congratulatory letters have arrived since she won the World Championship), hold meetings with her sponsors to try and fit in their requirements for visits for their clients, and arrange interviews with scores of reporters from all over the world who want her story. A favoured few journalists are invited to join her at Gatcombe for a friendly chat, while others just ring up if they have her mobile number. She is invariably polite and usually gives them a couple of minutes. If they are equestrian journalists, she will probably know them already and she is always willing to answer their questions, as they are knowledgeable about eventing and don't ring up just to find out the latest gossip about her love life.

By 7 a.m. in the winter, and earlier in the spring and summer, Zara will have arrived at the stables, which she calls the Pens. At her heels are her dogs: Misty, a bullmastiff, Sway, a boxer, and Corley, a Labrador. Waiting for her is Catherine Owen, her Head Girl, who has worked with Zara for five years and who comes from the Isle of Wight. Catherine, whose boyfriend is a policeman working in the security detail on the Gatcombe estate, accompanies Zara to competitions around the world, while Rachel Allardycc, who virtually runs the Pens, sometimes complains that she is always the one who is left behind to mind the shop when the other two are enjoying themselves. It is said jokingly, and they all know that each one is an integral part of the team, but in every team there can be only one captain and they all know that in this one it must be Zara.

Catherine is supportive of her boss but she also has to tell her things she would sometimes prefer not to, as when Toytown was injured. 'When Toytown hurt his leg in late 2003, she [Zara] was in Australia. I had to tell her and it was hard because he was her Olympic hope – for 18 months she had trained him for Athens. But she has her mother's attitude that you have to kick yourself back into touch . . . She's great fun and really cool. I'm the bossy one. She loves parties and she's not bitchy. But she gets upset by the way that some people seem to want her to fail.'

The only person at Gatcombe to whom Zara defers is her mother, and that is because she knows Mum has done it all before. But Princess Anne is careful to offer advice only when she is asked for it. She is not a domineering mother. Of course, the Princess, herself a former European Champion, will often be consulted about a particular equestrian point, and while Her Royal Highness has long retired from competing herself, her knowledge of the sport has proved invaluable to her daughter. She can see so much of herself in Zara that she knows the only way to get her to listen and take advice is to sit back and wait for questions. She will then answer Zara, but realises that it might take some time before her daughter acts on her advice. That is precisely the way Anne was when she was competing and Alison Oliver, her trainer, wanted to get a message across to her Royal pupil. Zara is self-willed, just like her mother, and if she thinks someone, even the Princess, is trying to make her do something she doesn't want to do, she digs her heels in and some members of her staff say she can be as stubborn as a mule. Everyone around her knows how to choose the right moment and how to gauge her mood at any particular time before offering advice.

Mark Phillips doesn't wait to be asked: he jumps in whenever he sees something that could be done better in his opinion. Zara and her father argue frequently over equestrian issues and she usually ends up agreeing that 'Father knows best'. He, in spite of being officially connected with the three day event team of the USA, still takes an active, paternal interest in his daughter's career and no one was more delighted than he when she won her world title. When she won the European Championship, Mark said, 'I couldn't have asked for more, I've never seen her ride better.' In addition to her mother and father, Zara will also consult her dressage coach, Sandy Pflueger, a former rider in the American team, who also happens to be her stepmother. So, it's all kept in the family.

Zara works with Catherine and Rachel mucking out and aims to have all the horses ridden every morning. Toytown is, of course, Zara's main concern but she also has three five-year-olds and a four-year-old: Tigerlilly, Trevor, Lili and Mickey, all of whom have to be worked throughout the year. As a result, the daily routine involves very early starts and incredibly long and tiring hours. When Zara says she needs to ride all her horses every day, it is not just a matter of hacking around a few fields and seeing to their feed and stables. She has a definite programme for each of them and they are worked in the truest sense of the word. Gatcombe has its own cross-country course, designed by Mark Phillips, and Zara uses it every day. The estate also has a dressage area and a show-jumping ring, so the training sessions are carried out under near-competition conditions. By the time she has ridden all of her horses, both she and they know they have done a day's work.

Yogi Breisner, the Great Britain Olympic equestrian team manager, believes that Mike and Zara 'inspire each other' and adds, 'Being with Mike really helps Zara because he is a dedicated sportsman.' Breisner does not have too much time for part-timers in his sport, or for those who do not take it as seriously as he does. 'There isn't too much time left for socialising,' he says. 'Top riders have to ride four to eight hours a day, every day and they have to be fit. Obviously, they don't want to put on weight, so anybody who is inclined to put on a few pounds [not a reference to Zara] has to watch their diet. In a world-class programme, we have nutritionists to help with diet, so there are no fry-ups for breakfast . . . You also have to start by 6.30 a.m., so you need to get to bed early to be fresh for the job ahead.' He also forbids mobile phones to be used during team training sessions, so if anyone rings up one of his riders, they have to go through him and he decides if the call is important enough to interfere with his strict programme.

At some point in the morning Zara tries to make a call at the big house where Margaret Hammond, one of the Princess Royal's Ladies-in-Waiting who also acts in an administrative capacity for Zara, will have gone through the day's post and filtered the enquiries that have come in since yesterday. Mrs Hammond, who has been made a Lieutenant of the Royal Victorian Order for her services to the Royal Family, is adept at knowing which interviews Zara wants to do, and she will have spoken to Susan McMahon, Zara's public relations adviser in her office in London. Zara also employs an agent, based in Australia, who handles a number of other leading equestrian stars and who is guiding her through the commercial labyrinth that her celebrity now attracts. There have been so many offers for her to endorse products that she has to be very careful in selecting those that will not reflect adversely on the Royal Family. No matter what she and her mother claim, companies want her not only for her sporting achievements but also, naturally, because of who her mother and grandmother are. No advertising manager worth his salt is going to pass up an opportunity like Zara, particularly when she is so newsworthy. And if she was highly sought after before she won the BBC Sports Personality of the Year Award in December 2006, her price went through the roof afterwards. The offers poured in and the day after the awards ceremony, she appeared in full-page advertisements for Land Rover as part of a series of very clever commercials showing her wearing an elegant evening gown, with the hem stained with mud. The ads were a brilliant combination of style and practicality, and showed the product at its best. Zara, and her agent and public relations adviser, had chosen well.

One rule that Zara follows religiously is that she will not wear the products of one of her sponsors when she is advertising one of the others. You will not see her sprawling on a Land Rover wearing a Rolex watch (Rolex was one of her earliest and most prestigious sponsors). What you will witness if you attend one of the major equestrian events of the year – Badminton, Burghley or Gatcombe – is Zara 'working the field' – in other words, visiting the stands of her sponsors, spending time with their clients and being photographed with them, always, of course, with the product prominently displayed. She knows the value of her name and she is prepared to exploit it, because as a competitor in one of the last truly amateur sports in the world, she needs the money from commercial sponsorship to be able to fund her activities.

Zara is not a great gourmet – just like her mother – so she eats sparingly. Lunch is often a very light affair of salad, fruit or cheese, and more frequently nothing at all. She is so wrapped up in her work that she nearly always forgets lunch altogether. And, of course, there is strictly no alcohol during the daytime. When she and Richard Johnson were together, they were often seen in a local pub having a pint of beer at lunchtime, but this was before Zara became seriously involved in eventing.

The afternoons are usually taken up with meetings arranged by her advisers and also by looking at the next day's programme with Margaret Hammond, who guards her diary. Zara sometimes joins her mother for afternoon tea, but it is not the same sort of feast that the Queen enjoys every day at 4.30 p.m. For the Phillips family, it is usually just a cup of tea and perhaps a toasted teacake.

Zara is still very close to her father – and also to her American stepmother, who both live on part of the Gatcombe estate, at Aston Farm. It is very convenient for everybody in the family, as Mark and his former wife still organise commercial shoots at Gatcombe, which raise very respectable sums, and Zara and Mark are able to see each other almost every day.

Another relation with whom Zara gets on very well is her cousin Prince William. When he is home on leave from the Army, he spends his weekends at Highgrove, which is just a couple of miles from Gatcombe, and he often joins Zara and Mike for a meal, sometimes in a local pub or restaurant but more frequently at their house. William is a great favourite of Zara's; they are practically the same age and share many of the same interests. He is a superb horseman and a great fan of the England rugby team. He was in Australia when Mike Tindall helped his country win the World Cup, so they obviously always have plenty to chat about. Zara is able to get away with murder with William. She is one of the few people who can tease him unmercifully and she never loses an opportunity to make him blush. When they, together with Prince Harry, were guests at the wedding of their uncle, Prince Edward, Earl of Wessex, to Sophie Rhys-Jones in 1999 at Windsor Castle, their table was far and away the noisiest at the reception. Even the Queen, sitting some distance away, remarked on how much they seemed to be enjoying themselves. That was her way of saying they were causing too much of a disturbance. But Zara failed miserably when she tried to drag William onto the dance floor. He adamantly refused to get up, in spite of her threats and pleas. He said he was not going to make an exhibition of himself just to please her. Nevertheless, they remain the best of friends and are probably the closest of all the younger Royals.

Mike Tindall gets home around 5.30 p.m. and he and Zara meet to chat over the day's events and decide what they are going to do in the evening. They sometimes argue over who is going to have first use of the bathroom – with Mike's formidable size, they cannot manage to bathe together (unless it is in the outside hot tub) – and Mike usually lets Zara win.

He and Zara both love television. If she misses an episode of her favourite 'soap', someone usually records it for her to watch at a later date. The couple also like sports programmes, particularly quiz shows like the BBC's *A Question of Sport*, on which they appeared together, but on opposing teams. Once again it was a case of Zara following in her mother's footsteps, as Princess Anne appeared on the show in 1987, when she was a great hit with the England soccer star Emlyn Hughes.

At the end of the day both Zara and Mike are usually exhausted. Her working day often lasts for fourteen hours or more. Members of her staff say she works unbelievably hard, and she never goes to bed without first checking on all the horses late at night. No matter what the time of night or the weather, she always goes across to the stables to see that everything is in order and that her 'babies' are bedded down. Then, and only then, can she go to sleep herself.

It's a tough life, but one she has chosen for herself and it seems to suit her. She knows last thing at night that tomorrow it will all start again.

10 CHAMPION OF EUROPE

After competing at trials in England and Europe since 2001, Zara was starting to make an impact on the equestrian scene. She was yet to win a major competition, but she had been placed several times and her father said there were a number of occasions when she could have won if only she had maintained her concentration.

At the Windsor Three Day Event in 2001, Zara was in the lead going into the final show-jumping round but dropped to 33rd place after having no fewer than six fences down. It was the worst show-jumping she had ever done and her mother let her know it in no uncertain terms. Princess Anne and Zara had what would diplomatically be called a 'frank and vigorous exchange of views'. The Princess sees no point in glossing over faults; either her own or anyone else's, and she was angry and disappointed that her daughter had let herself down in such an unnecessary fashion.

This was when Mark Phillips took over the coaching of his daughter in show-jumping. Toytown was already an accomplished cross-country horse, so they didn't need to spend too much time there, just a little fine-tuning. It was in show-jumping that there was the most need, and by 2002 the hard work by Mark, Zara and Toytown started to pay dividends.

Zara was successful in the Under-25 Championships at the Bramham Horse Trials in 2002 and then in September of that year, travelled to Austria to take part in the European Young Riders Championships. Some horses do not travel well, but Toytown has no problem, and he and Zara won the individual silver medal at the championships. People were starting to sit up and take notice. But it was the following year, 2003, when she made her first appearance at Burghley, where her mother had won her European crown in 1971, that Zara announced to the world of equestrianism that she was a force to be reckoned with.

The cross-country course at Burghley was demanding for even the most experienced riders and horses, but Zara encountered few problems and at the end of the phase she was in the lead. She should have won, but once again her show-jumping let her down. She knocked one fence over, which meant she came in second place to Pippa Funnell, her great heroine, who took the Rolex Grand Prix. Despite her show-jumping, Zara's performance had announced that she was ready for the big time and able to compete with the world's best on equal terms.

For the moment, Zara had reached a new high, but shortly afterwards she was brought sharply back to earth and the euphoria quickly disappeared, as she suffered a massive disappointment and setback. Toytown received a leg injury in the winter, ruling them both out of a possible place in the British team to compete in the 2004 Olympic Games in Athens. They would have been almost certain to gain a place because of their high placing at Burghley, but none of Zara's other horses was anywhere near the standard required to challenge for a place in the British squad.

Looking back on the disappointment, Zara now feels it was probably a blessing in disguise, although she didn't feel that way as she sat watching the games on television, wondering what she and Toytown might have achieved. Toytown was a light horse with a weak back and the year he had away from competition improved his overall condition immensely. With hindsight, Zara thought that missing Athens was arguably the best thing that could have happened to both of them for their long-term career.

Putting this setback behind her and taking second place on Toytown at Luhmuhlen in June 2005 was enough for Zara to be selected, as an individual, for the European Trials three months later. But following the withdrawal of Primmores Pride, Zara was promoted to a place in the official British team, replacing the experienced Pippa Funnell. The rest is history.

Zara was thrilled to be selected, particularly as she was the baby of the team, being only 24, with the next youngest team member twelve years older. The rest of the four-man team: William Fox-Pitt, Jeanette Brakewell and Leslie Law, were far more experienced than their newest recruit. Law was an Olympic gold medallist and the others were seasoned international competitors. Great Britain were the defending champions, having won the event for the previous five successive years, but the last-minute injury to Pippa Funnell's leading horse meant they did not enter the competition as favourites to retain the title. Zara said she was surprised to be selected for the team, but Pippa Funnell wasn't. 'If I was a selector, I would have chosen Zara,' she said.

Zara won the European Three Day Event title on 11 September 2005, 24 years after her mother had won the same championship. Zara's triumph came at Blenheim Palace, birthplace of Winston Churchill, and she showed she was one of the outstanding riders of her generation in coping with some of the worst weather conditions ever experienced in the competition.

In the initial phase of dressage, Zara rode into contention on Toytown, managing a creditable equal third place with Germany's Frank Ostholt on Air Jordan. Bettina Hoy on Ringwood Cockatoo was the leader, and Pippa Funnell, who, in spite of having to withdraw from the British team, was able to compete as an individual with her second string, Ensign, rode brilliantly to secure second place. All together there were twelve British riders taking part (four in the official team) and the British manager, Yogi Breisner, told of his pleasure at the way all the Britons had performed. 'I don't think any of them could have gone any better,' he said. At the end of the first phase, Germany was in the lead with a 12.2 advantage over Britain, but all that meant was they could afford to have only one refusal in the cross-country section. It was during that phase, ridden over four miles of tortuous track, that Zara showed her true mettle.

The cross-country phase took place during a continuous, torrential downpour that made conditions treacherous for horse and rider, and at some points on the course visibility was down to just a few yards. Riders could barely see how far ahead the next fence was. The course was greasy and the early riders found it difficult to finish inside the time allowed.

The British team got off to a faultless start when Jeanette Brakewell and the seventeen-year-old Over to You rode a magnificent clear round within the time, making up twelve places on her dressage score. William Fox-Pitt and his tiny horse, Tamarillo, made the course look deceptively easy and there were comments that the designer, the experienced Michael Etherington-Smith, who was also commissioned to design the cross-country course for the 2008 Beijing Olympic Games, had perhaps made the course at Blenheim a little too easy for the better riders and horses. But Mike's course proved more difficult for some riders. Bettina Hoy, who had scored 31.3 in the dressage test to put her in gold medal position, had a disastrous round when Ringwood Cockatoo decided he didn't like the look of Cameron's Cottage, a deceptively innocent-looking obstacle built to look like a house on top of a steep run down to the water. He dug in his heels and Bettina had to have a second attempt at the fence, which meant she collected 20 penalties and was out of the running for an individual medal. The reigning European Champion, Nicholas Touzaint, fell from grace in more ways than one when he took a tumble into the water from Hildago de L'ile, and his championship hopes were dashed.

The anchor of the British team, Leslie Law and Shear L'eau finished clear but incurred time penalties. Law had to nurse his mount, hero of the Athens Olympics, around the course after nearly having a fall at the nineteenth, while Pippa Funnell was delirious when her former racehorse, Ensign, also went clear with only a few time penalties, to enable her to retain her second place as an individual.

Before she entered the phase, Zara said there was no fence on the course where you could take it easy – they were all a problem. One of her fellow competitors said later that as far as Zara was concerned obstacles weren't obstacles, but challenges, and Toytown, described by his former owner Meryl Winter as a 'cross-country machine', obviously relished the prospect of attacking the course. The horse has never shown the slightest hesitation over the most hazardous obstacles and Blenheim was to prove no different.

It took not only clinical analytical skills to negotiate the course but also tremendous courage. Zara proved she possessed both in abundance by riding a clear round that took her into the lead. While the majority of riders finished with clear rounds, only eight managed it inside the time. She was soaked to the skin as she finished and when she entered the ring for the show-jumping phase on the Sunday afternoon, her boots were still wet.

The closeness of the scores after the cross-country meant a nail-biting finish was a possibility on the final day, and the show-jumping would decide the winner. Zara was in the individual lead after the dressage and cross-country sections, but the result was never a foregone conclusion. She was going to need all her skill and determination to remain among the medals. Her team-mate William Fox-Pitt, with Tamarillo, had already gone clear, as had Germany's Ingrid Klimke with her horse, Sleep Late.

It made no difference. Zara had the slight cushion of being able to knock down one fence and still win, but she didn't need it. After another clear round within the time, Zara was number one in Europe. She had shown amazing composure for someone so new to the senior ranks of three day events.

Zara caused a few near heart attacks among the British contingent, especially her mother and father who were both watching in the crowd, when she rattled a few of the twelve fences on her way around. Fortunately she didn't dislodge any. She later said, 'I could hear Toytown tapping some, and this helped me to concentrate even more. But the crowd were wonderful and supportive, urging me on.' She added, 'I did rattle a couple but I think that's quite good because if you don't touch them you get a bit casual.'

As she received her trophy from her proud and delighted mother, Zara was still in a daze and didn't realise fully that she was the new champion. After all, just a year earlier she had been ranked a lowly 36th in the world, so at the start of the competition she was not really expected to win. Even though, in 2003, Pippa Funnell had beaten Zara to first place at the Burghley Horse Trials, on this occasion Pippa, on her second horse Ensign, had made two mistakes in the show-jumping round and dropped from second to ninth at the finish. Fox-Pitt took the silver medal and Germany's Klimke, the bronze.

Zara's triumph at Blenheim was doubled when she received not one, but two gold medals, the second as a member of the official British Team. The team silver went to France, who had managed to overhaul Germany. Zara later said she loved being part of the team and was very proud of riding for Britain. It was her first experience of being in the British squad at senior level and the support from the openly partisan crowd was, in her words, 'truly amazing'. She said it was the best experience of her life to hear the crowds all the way round the cross-country course, cheering her and the other team members at every step and at every fence. What was so incredible about her victory was the way she had handled Toytown in such a mature fashion for one so young and inexperienced. Watching her in the dressage, cross-country and final show-jumping sections, one would have been forgiven for thinking that here was a rider to whom top-class, international competitions were an everyday experience. In all honesty, any of the other members of the British team – and several of the individual riders – would have been favourites to win over Zara, and it speaks volumes for the *esprit de corps* of British equestrianism that no one begrudged her her moment of triumph. They were all delighted at her success and welcomed their newest – and youngest – member, into the higher echelons of three day eventing.

It had been a wonderful day for British riding, and less than a year later, there was even better to come.

Zara spoke emotionally after the awards ceremony. Proudly wearing her two gold medals, she said, 'It has always been a massive dream to win gold like this. It is so bizarre to think I have one more than my mother, but it is even better to have a team gold. It has been an honour and a privilege to ride with Jeanette Breakwell, William [Fox-Pitt], and Leslie Law.'

Recalling the events of that day, Zara tells the story of the Queen's reaction. 'My grandmother was up in Scotland [at Balmoral] watching the TV coverage of me at Blenheim. On television there was a five-minute delay between the live action and the broadcast. Anyway, Mum phoned her up immediately after I'd jumped clear to tell her the news that I'd just won the European title. My grandmother's first response was to go, "Shush, I'm still watching it now." I think Mum spoiled the ending for her.'

The general public showed their approval of Zara's achieve-ments when they voted her *Sunday Times* Sportswoman of the Year. In a ceremony in November 2005, held in Old Billingsgate Market in London, Zara received her trophy, beating off stiff competition from the record-breaking athlete Paula Radcliffe and round-the-world sailor Dame Ellen MacArthur. What was particularly pleasing for Zara was that this award came from members of the public. And it also meant that her sport was once again being recognised along with the more traditional sports of rugby, soccer, tennis and athletics.

Zara rapidly discovered that one of the penalties – if you can call it that – of sudden fame, is that you become public property overnight and everyone feels they have a right to a part of you. Zara coped well with it and didn't suffer from what some famous people call 'celebrity-fatigue'. She didn't mind a bit when members of the public approached her and never refused a request for an autograph, though it took a little getting used to in the beginning, when she found it a bit embarrassing.

She was walking around Gatcombe during an event held there shortly after she won the European title, stopping at various stands, chatting to the stall-holders and buying the odd item or two, when she was approached by two rather shy young girls who asked if they could take her photograph. Zara agreed and said she had a better idea, calling her companion over and asking him to take her picture with the girls. They were thrilled and delighted. Later they sent her a print of the photograph, asking her to sign it. She did so and added a personal greeting before posting it back to them. It made their day and gave them something they will remember for many years. How many celebrities would have gone to so much trouble for two young strangers?

Victory in Europe had given Zara a new confidence. No longer was she hesitant about her ability in the show-jumping ring. She now knew she had no need to be afraid of anyone – or any venue. While she had not lacked courage before, it was nice to have this major triumph under her belt as she planned her next move.

11 ON TOP OF THE WORLD

Zara Phillips made history in August 2006 when she won the eventing individual gold medal and world title at the World Equestrian Games in Aachen, Germany, a festival founded by her grandfather, the Duke of Edinburgh.

She had virtually clinched her victory by the close of the second day, during the testing cross-country course, which was described as a 'true World Championship track' by every rider in the competition. Zara's former coach, Bettina Hoy, riding for the host country, entered the phase in lead position after a brilliant dressage performance. But, even though she had a clear round on the cross-country course, she incurred 7.2 time faults by playing it safe and going the long way round at two of the most technical fences.

World titles are not won by playing it safe, and Zara made sure when her turn came that she would not do so. She rode sensationally, taking the shortest and straightest route that even more experienced riders shied away from. It was an object lesson in aggressive, attacking riding, with Zara behaving exactly as both of her parents did when they were competing at international level, and she completed the course well inside the allotted time, with a clear round.

The Great Britain team comprised Zara Phillips on Toytown, Daisy Dick on Spring Along, William Fox-Pitt on Tamarillo and Mary King on Call Again Cavalier, with several other British riders, including the seasoned Oliver Townend, riding as individuals. Zara was the youngest, and by far the least experienced rider in the British team, with virtually no international experience, but what she lacked in experience she more than made up for in aggressive riding and sheer talent.

Zara was told of her selection for the British team in March 2006, so she had five months to get used to the idea and to plan her training programme accordingly. She admitted to being nervous before Aachen, saying, 'Of course, I worry before each event. My way of dealing with it is to run through everything I have to do in my head first.' She added that keeping Toytown in peak condition was her main aim in the months leading up to Aachen.

What was so brilliant about Aachen was the British team spirit. They all supported each other, there was no backbiting and they took their meals together, with the senior members mixing with the most junior – among them Zara – in a totally informal manner. Yogi Breisner, the manager of the team, even had the dinner-table settings deliberately mixed up so that old and new sat together.

The British *chef d'equipe* issued a handbook to everyone in the team. It laid down what he believed to be the crucial ingredients of success, including 'honesty, integrity, loyalty and confidentiality'. The handbook was given to everyone, not only the riders but also to the grooms and support staff. It made them all feel they were an integral part of the team. Breisner has been manager of the British team since 2000 and under his guidance they have won medals every year since. The riders say he is every bit as competitive as they are and has the ability to get the best out of his people. As a former Olympic rider himself – he represented Sweden at Los Angeles in 1984 – Yogi knows exactly what his riders are going through, and they all say they would be lost without him.

The dressage phase is generally regarded by laymen as the most boring of the three disciplines in three day events, simply because it is carried out in complete silence with all instructions to the horse being given through the legs and hands of the rider. It is fascinating to those who understand the complicated moves required but it is usually only the purists who remain glued to their seats for the entire day's performance. The concentration needed to maintain a high-level performance is very demanding – and having to control a horse while wearing a top hat doesn't make it any easier. However, it is one thing to ride a good dressage and quite another to withstand the pressures of the cross-country course, when a clear round in excellent time is obligatory if one is to be in contention on the final day.

Germany's Bettina Hoy, who had coached Zara for a time in dressage, was the favourite and she produced her customary brilliant performance to take and hold the lead on her horse, Ringwood Cockatoo, with 36.50 points. In second place was her team-mate, Ingrid Klimke on Sleep Late with 39.10 points. Germany also occupied third place, with Andreas Dibowski on Serve Well.

Great Britain were not too downhearted at the end of day one, as there had been a splendid performance from the newcomer, Zara Phillips on Toytown, putting her into fifth place with 41.70 points, ahead of William Fox-Pitt and Tamarillo in eighth.

Ahead lay the toughest section, the cross-country course, built by one of Germany's leading course designers, Rüdiger Schwartz. It was his first World Championship course and it was highly praised by every rider and also by the 44,000 spectators who lined the track at Soers. He explained what he had been trying to do with his course design. 'My fundamental idea was to make sure that the best pairs headed the field in the World Championships. I placed all the obstacles that are very technical and demand a great deal of freshness from the rider and horse at the start of the course. Towards the end, when the concentration starts to fade, I opted for elements which test the honesty and strength of the horse. I think I achieved that aim quite well.' Schwartz's concept worked brilliantly. Although every rider said the course was demanding and technical, they all agreed it was fair and fitting for a World Championship.

A field of 76 competitors set off around the course of 31 natural obstacles (45 fences), and 59 managed to finish. Seven retired and ten were eliminated after refusals or a fall. Happily, there were no serious falls, with only one rider, the Australian Sonja Johnson, being taken to hospital with suspected concussion, which turned out to be just bruising. The cross-country course saw a complete upset of the formbook, with only four of the top ten riders from the dressage phase managing clear rounds.

In the British team, Daisy Dick on Spring Along took the alternative, longer route but still managed to finish inside the time, but Mary King on Call Again Cavalier glanced off the angled first element of the final water jump. Another clear round came from Oliver Townend on Flint Curtis, even though he later commented, 'Neither of us has seen a course like that before.' One of the star performers in the British team, William Fox-Pitt, caused a huge upset of the formbook when he failed at Fence 15, the Normandy Bank. He apologised later, saying, 'I am so sorry for the team after Daisy and Zara's brilliant clears.'

'My horse did a fantastic job,' a thrilled Zara declared after her wonderful clear round. 'Of course, there were a few hairy moments, and I could have jumped the first water better, but I am very pleased. I went for the straight routes everywhere, it was the simplest thing to do. The course was fabulous to ride and Rüdiger Schwartz deserves a lot of praise. I can hardy believe I am in the lead.' Toytown, the chestnut English gelding, showed what a true thoroughbred he was. Zara's clear round had put the British team into silver medal position after some of the brilliantly conceived obstacles had caught out many of the early favourites.

Bettina Hoy, who was now in second place after leading the dressage, said she was happy with her performance. 'I felt Cockatoo was getting a bit tired towards the end and I decided to take two alternative routes to secure a clear round for the German team.' This was a strategy agreed before the competition began. Zara and Bettina live just a few miles from each other in Gloucestershire and they have been friends for years. After the cross-country course was completed, Bettina said, 'We don't compete against each other, we compete against the course. Whoever wins . . . will be a worthy World Champion.'

There were only eleven clear rounds in this speed and endurance test; three for Germany and two for Great Britain, and at the end of the day, Zara was in the lead going into the final phase, show-jumping. This is the section she had always loathed, believing she could not do it successfully. It was her father who finally persuaded her that the fears were all in her mind and she should put these problems aside and concentrate.

The first two days had been closely fought and any one of several riders could have won the gold medal. The show-jumping phase was just as close, with Bettina Hoy and Frank Ostler, both representing Germany, lying a close second and third at the start of the day. Everyone, not just the partisan home crowd, believed the gold medal was destined to remain on German soil. Zara had other ideas and when Ostler had one fence down and Bettina Hoy had two plus a time fault, the only hope for Germany was if Zara had a worse round. The Gatcombe winner, Clayton Fredericks, jumped a magnificent clear round which would win him the silver medal. All five British jumpers jumped cleanly, with just one time fault for Sharon Hunt and two for Oliver Townend. Even so, it was a nerve-wracking wait for Zara, as she had less than one fence in hand over the vastly more experienced Bettina Hoy.

The stadium at Aachen is massive and the event horses had not seen anything of that size before, so Zara had a lot to prove, both to herself and to the rest of the British team. None of her compatriots was in the running for the gold medal and all hopes were on her young shoulders. She may have had the advantage of being in the lead as she entered the ring, but the ultra-partisan home crowd were convinced that, with their help, local favourite Bettina Hoy could bring the gold medal back to Germany. Their team was already in first place with Britain in the silver medal position.

Before the show-jumping phase began, Zara was asked how she felt. She replied, 'Hopefully that big arena will lift him. For the riders it will be daunting, but I'm really looking forward to it.' Before the World Championships, Zara and Toytown had only jumped one clear show-jumping round that year – and they had incurred time faults even then. There was a lot to prove, but her last clear round before Aachen was the last one she had jumped, so perhaps that was a good omen.

As the leading rider, Zara was last out in the show-jumping ring, which meant an anxious wait to see the scores she would have to beat. To add to the pressure, there was so much noise from the 30,000 spectators who had packed the arena as she waited for her turn, and who had just heard the announcement that Germany had won the team gold, that Zara didn't hear the bell so she did not get to the start on time.

Afterwards Zara said, 'I didn't hear the starting bell, so I tried looking at the clock as I circled. That's why I was late and hence my time faults.' There was a lot to make up but she displayed immense composure during her round. There were big distances between the fences and a 95-second time limit for the course, a time that was too short for many of the experienced riders who went before Zara. But Zara rode with a smoothness and elegance that belied her youth and inexperience and settled down to prove that she was going to enjoy herself and not be thrown by the noise of the crowd.

As she approached the final fences she looked up at the clock to check how she was doing. Before the final two fences, Zara and Toytown were clear. They clipped the final part of the penultimate fence, causing the British contingent to gasp, but then cleared the final fence. Zara said later that she rushed that last fence, but she had a single fence in hand and completed a brilliant round. The title was hers.

She had scored 46.70 points, just 2 points ahead of the second-placed rider, Australian Clayton Fredericks on Ben Along Time, with the American Amy Tryon in third place on

Poggio with 50.70 points. Just four points separated the first three places; such is the closeness of competition at this level. Germany had won no individual medals; their riders took fourth, fifth and sixth places.

After she was presented with her gold medal, Zara said, 'It was amazing to jump in that arena. Eventers have never seen anything like it. My horse felt great and I was confident in him. He loves crowds and thinks they are there for him. I just had to get myself right. And I am so relieved and happy to get through it. I really did enjoy it, even if I did not look like it.'

By any standards it was a fantastic result, both for Great Britain and for Zara. But the victory was tinged with sadness as Zara's friend, the Northern Ireland rider Sherelle Duke, had died one week earlier after falling from her horse and having the animal fall on top of her during trials at Brockenhurst. Sherelle had been hoping to be part of the British team in Aachen, and Zara dedicated her win to her friend, saying, 'I dedicate this victory to my friend who passed away last week.' Zara had wanted to attend Sherelle's funeral, but the team were already in Germany and the manager asked them all to remain. The British and Irish teams competed wearing red and white ribbons, Sherelle's cross-country colours, in memory of her. Zara had promised Sherelle's family and her boyfriend, who all fully understood the reason why she couldn't be present at the funeral, that she would win a gold medal as a tribute to her friend – and she kept her word.

It was after her win in Aachen that Zara first spoke of how the death of her good friend had affected her. 'Yogi [Breisner] told us, and for the first few days I was very miserable and anti-social ... Sherelle was a beautiful person and a great rider, and she knew what Toytown was capable of. So I was determined to try to win for her.' Sherelle was a very special friend of Zara's and she had stayed with her at Gatcombe on a number of occasions, so it wasn't just another competitor who had died. Zara felt her death as a personal loss. The tragedy also made Zara realise how lucky she had been to escape serious injury over the years.

Germany won the overall team title at the World Championships with 156 points, with Britain in second place, followed by Australia in the bronze medal position. Zara had beaten 78 of the best riders in the world to win the championship; it really was an 'amazing' (to use her word) result.

While the top three German riders filled places four, five and six individually, their primary focus had always been the team event. Their fifth-placed rider, Heinrich Romeike, praised Zara's win when he said, 'I think it's great that the World Championship hasn't been won by a dressage horse or a show-jumper,' a reference to the fact that Toytown is primarily a cross-country event horse. Most three day event riders say the cross-country section is the toughest of all three disciplines and they are usually pleased when this phase decides the winner.

Shortly before she left for Aachen, Zara said, 'People think I am privileged because of my parents. It's a label that's hard to shift, but the people who say that don't know me.' And with a reference to previous tabloid revelations about her love-life, she once remarked, 'What I really want from doing well at competitions is to be recognised for riding, not for who my grandmother is or for what's going on in my personal life.'

Before the World Championship, Zara, along with the other members of the British team, had been asked to fill in a questionnaire about their likes and dislikes. She revealed that one of her superstitions was that she has to wear the same socks when she rides cross-country, and that the rider she most admires is Pippa Funnell. 'She has got it all worked out and has worked really hard to get where she is,' Zara said. Pippa is the outstanding name in British three day events, with three Badminton wins, and she is the only rider to have won the Rolex Grand Slam: Kentucky, Badminton and Burghley in succession. Zara admitted that show-jumping was her least favourite part of a three day event and that Burgie in Scotland is her favourite venue because 'it is so relaxed and you are so well looked after.'

After the competition ended, Will Connell, *chef de mission* for the British team, told of his pride and pleasure at the results. 'There are three things that made the eventing so special for Team GB. The first is Zara's individual gold, and the professional job that she did; the second is team silver – yes, William and Mary are annoyed at the mistakes they had and of course we wish we had got gold, but second in the world isn't bad! But thirdly, and most importantly, is the fact that we did it with a new team. It's the first time we've brought out a team that didn't include Pippa Funnell or Jeanette Brakewell, and they did fantastically. It shows eventing is moving forward.' He also mentioned that it was particularly pleasing that the youngest member of the British team had won the individual gold medal.

Zara had proved that she was a champion – the best in the world. Her father had some early doubts that she had it in her to win at all costs, something that separates the merely talented from the great. She proved him wrong in Aachen, and he was delighted that she was able to do so. Zara proved beyond any doubt that she possesses not only the right attitude, but also the killer instinct, and that the pursuit of excellence in sport is nothing to be ashamed of. She gave no quarter to any of her rivals, asked for none in return, and only when the final phase was finished did she let down her guard and allow her emotions to show.

Throughout the competition Zara had kept her cool. She had been under enormous pressure but she was used to it, having spent several years before she arrived in Aachen competing with the additional handicap of having to do all her learning under the constant gaze of a hyper-critical public and with press cameras practically jammed right under her nose at all times. No other rider, apart from her mother 35 years earlier, had had to learn the business of eventing with every move photographed and commented upon.

But, outwardly laid back, with a warm-spirited natural grace that conceals the Mountbatten-Windsor spine of steel, Zara was ready and able to cope when she was criticised as being just another little rich kid with a Princess for a mother and a Queen for a grandmother, who could buy her anything – even a world title. She knew what she had had to do to achieve her success – and her team-mates acknowledged that being Royal had nothing to do with it. One of them said, 'If people only knew the endless hours of practice that Zara puts in on all three disciplines to perfect her performance, they might not be so quick to criticise.'

Zara's success owed much to the coaching she had received from the best of British, American, German, Australian and Swedish equestrian experts. Each contributed in his or her own style and Zara fully justified their faith. She followed their instructions (almost) to the letter, just occasionally showing that streak of independence so reminiscent of her mother. Princess Anne took up eventing to show she could do something well in her own right, without the 'Royal' tag, and Zara did it for the same reason. They both like the smell of danger and to live on the edge.

Zara's parents had been in Aachen to see their daughter's triumph, and afterwards the Princess Royal, who is not given to extravagant praise, told Zara she had done a 'fabulous job' after the cross-country, and when she won the world title, said she was 'very pleased'. This was 'Princess Royal-speak' for being over the moon.

Zara had travelled to Germany accompanied by her brother Peter. They had driven all the way from Gatcombe, and were going home by the same route. They were both starving after the event and one of Zara's sponsors, James Blackshaw, of Cantor Index, who has become a close friend since their professional relationship has blossomed, was the last person to wave Zara and Peter off from Aachen. As they hadn't had anything to eat, and they couldn't afford the time to stop, he boxed up a couple of pizzas for them to enjoy en route to Calais and the late-night ferry across the Channel. No stretch limousines and champagne for this latest world-beater. That would all come later.

Two weeks after her triumph, Zara returned to Aachen as guest of honour at a celebratory Dinner of Champions, which concluded the World Equestrian Games. At the start of the games, Zara would have been thrilled just to be among the leaders; now she had proved she was the best, and it felt wonderful.

Later, she took Toytown to Burghley, not to compete this time but just to show him, as so many people wanted to see the new World Champion. And it was there that she revealed how she had come close to giving up the sport altogether after winning the European Championships in 2005. 'My other horses were going so badly, and I was riding so badly, that I thought I didn't want to do it anymore. People thought that, as the European Champion, I should be enjoying it. But I wasn't.'

She added that it was Pippa Funnell who persuaded her to carry on. Zara had been brought into the British team for the European Championship only because of an injury to Pippa's horse. Zara said, 'I spoke to Pippa because she had been through it and she told me to go away for a week and do something different. So I did that, came back and started concentrating on the World Championships. It still seems amazing. It was my first time in a World Championships, my first time in Aachen. It was very exciting. I am lucky to have such a good horse.' Zara admitted that having Mike Tindall in Aachen had helped her. 'He is very laid back, good to have around and a calming influence,' she said. And when a reporter asked her if Toytown was the love of her life, she laughed and said, 'Yes, but don't tell Mike.'

Following her victory, the plaudits flowed in from all over the equestrian world. Her peers were unanimous in their praise for her win. Richard Meade, arguably Britain's greatest ever three day event rider, with four Olympic gold medals, said, 'Zara's victory at Aachen was a tremendous achievement. To win both the European and World titles within the space of twelve months is outstanding. Zara proved beyond all doubt that she has got what it takes and she really is a most talented rider.' He added, 'Zara has a wonderful major competition temperament. Many riders look good and perform well at small meetings, but go to pieces when it is the big occasion. Zara coped well at the most difficult of the lot, the World Championships. They don't come any harder.' Referring to Toytown, he added, 'He knew he had a brilliant rider on his back and she knew exactly what she had to do. I cannot see any reason why she cannot continue successfully for many years to come.'

Meade confessed that when he was riding in competition, he hated to lose. 'It wasn't just I felt taking part was good enough. If I didn't win when I thought I should have, I blamed myself and went through every moment of the event to see what I had done wrong. Losing was something I never became used to and fortunately it didn't happen all that often. I think that is part of the secret of Zara's success. She knows she has to win and, like me, she hates the very idea of losing. I think, in her case, it is what separates the great from the merely good.'

A month after winning the world title, another accolade was added to her impressive string of achievements when she was named as HOYS [Horse of the Year Show's] Equestrian of the Year. Having beaten the world's best, it was perhaps inevitable that she would win, and she was presented with the handsome trophy, which depicts a grey horse on a globe, in a ceremony that was filmed and shown later when the Horse of the Year Show took place at the Birmingham National Exhibition Centre. The HOYS trophy is traditionally awarded for unique achievements by an individual or team in the equestrian world across all disciplines. Zara's heroine, Pippa Funnell, had been among previous winners and Zara's award was recognition of her unsurpassed performance in Aachen.

In December of that year, Zara won even more awards: four in the space of fourteen days. One of the most prestigious was the BEWA Trophy awarded by the British Equestrian Writers' Association. What was so pleasing about this prize was that it was the first time in the association's 34-year history that the award had been given by a unanimous vote by all its members. Receiving the trophy, Zara said, 'It is incredible winning all these awards, and I have to thank a lot of people, including my papa, who is the bane of my life. And Sandy. I would also like to thank my groom, Catherine

Owen, without whom I couldn't do anything. She never takes a holiday.'

The year 2006 may have been Zara's most successful in the saddle, but it ended on the operating table. She revealed that towards the end of the year she had needed urgent surgery. 'Just after Christmas I had to have my appendix out. It hadn't burst, but was right up by my kidney, and was pretty manky when they took it out,' she said.

Zara, who is bursting with robust health, soon recovered, and within weeks of the New Year she and Toytown had joined the other top British riders at a training session at the Unicorn Trust at Stow-on-the-Wold in preparation of the defence of her European title in Italy in September. Zara said this was something she was really looking forward to, feeling no more pressure than anyone else just because she was the one to beat in 2007.

As soon as Zara won the world title, people were speculating about her making it a triple crown: European, World and Olympic in 2008. Britain are the current holders of the individual Olympic gold medal through Leslie Law, and he might have something to say about his young rival's ambitions. He certainly isn't going to relinquish his crown without a fight.

12 ROYAL PURSUIT

Ever since the death of Diana, Princess of Wales, the press and the public have been searching for a young, present-able Royal who combines good looks with friendly attributes. It seems that Diana's sons, Princes William and Harry, are being groomed to become popular with the people, but the Queen knows there is also a need for a young woman to join 'The Firm' and provide a female balance to the Princes. The press are promoting Zara to fill that vacancy. She ticks all the right boxes, and once she has her immediate equestrian ambitions out of the way, she might well be the next Diana.

Zara has been news for one reason or another since the day she was born. When she was a small child, it was because she was the first granddaughter of the Queen. Then when she was just eight years old, her parents hit the headlines by announcing their separation (the first separation followed by divorce of one of the sovereign's children, though two more were to follow). Many of the articles that appeared at the time of the announcement concentrated on the effect the separation might have on Zara and her brother.

At one time the situation between Zara and the media got to the point where she felt she had to defend herself. She spoke out, saying she would not wish the unremitting glare of non-stop publicity on her worst enemy. She hated being called a 'Royal Rebel', claiming she was neither of these things. She was wrong on one count of course; whether she likes it or not, she is Royal, but the 'Rebel' description is open to question. The appellation was a tabloid invention and the papers were accused of double standards, saying that on the one hand they criticised the Queen and other members of the family as being 'fuddy-duddies', who were completely out of touch with the modern world, while at the same time having a go at Zara for behaving in a manner in keeping with other young people of her generation. Zara now has a more resigned attitude towards the 'Royal Rebel' tag. She knows it is never going to go away, and no matter what she does, even if she is chosen for the 2008 Olympic Games, someone will still refer to her by that description. There's nothing she can do about it, so she just grins and bears it.

Since Zara's affair with Richard Johnson, which was well documented by the press, she has made headlines in just about every newspaper in the country, and many overseas. Sometimes this is because of her love-life, while on other occasions the focus is on her clothing. As long ago as March 2003, the *Sun* ran the following headline above a picture of her at the races: ZARA PHILLIPS SHOWS SHE IS FURLONGS AHEAD IN THE STYLE STAKES. Every Christmas she is featured in photographs taken at Sandringham with other members of the Royal Family, but the caption under her picture inevitably refers to what she is wearing, especially if she is sporting a mini-skirt.

Other headlines over the years have included: RACY ZARA IS A TOP FILLY, ZARA: I'M NO WILD CHILD, CROCKED ZARA COMFORTED (when she fell off her horse and her boyfriend of the moment put his arm around her), ZARA RAPS 'ROYAL' REBEL TAG, ZARA TAKES ON TIPPLESTARS, and CROWN JEWELS, when she wore an evening gown that revealed her 'prize assets'.

Like many celebrities, Zara is ambivalent about her press coverage. On one hand she craves privacy when it suits her; on the other, she gets annoyed if something she has done that she feels is worthy of favourable attention does not get anywhere near the newspaper column inches she wants. In this she differs from her mother, who would be quite happy never to appear in a newspaper article or to have her photograph published in a magazine. That said, Princess Anne did cooperate with the present author when he was writing her biography many years ago.

Zara's first cousin, Prince William, is the young Royal upon whom most press attention is focussed these days. He is regarded, quite rightly, as the star of the future and the media need someone of his status, and undoubted good looks, to fill the gap left by his late mother. Unfortunately for the press, he refuses to play the game. He is more 'streetwise' than his father was at his age, and he has seen what an intrusive media can do. He still won't forgive them for what he regards as the appalling way they treated his late mother, Diana, Princess of Wales. When it was pointed out to William by his father's press office that he couldn't have it both ways – that he must either learn to cope with the attention or stay away from those places where the photographers knew he was going to be – he simply ignored their advice. No one was going to tell him where he could and could not go.

The rest of the younger generation of Royals do not warrant anywhere near the same amount of coverage as William. They can go wherever they like, with whomever they wish and few photographers bother them. Pictures of the Duke of York's daughters, Princesses Beatrice and Eugenie, appear from time to time, but mainly to show how they are growing up, not because they are particularly newsworthy in their own right. Their mother, the Duchess of York, is still considered good value by the media, providing pictures and stories that are guaranteed to find exposure in the papers, especially when she is wearing one of her more 'interesting' outfits.

When Peter and Zara Phillips were born, there was tremendous excitement at first and it was anticipated that they would attract fantastic media attention as they grew up. Fortunately for them it didn't happen on any large scale, or at least not until fairly recently in Zara's case, when her sporting celebrity and her love life began to attract attention. The Princess

Royal's decision not to allow her children to be given titles when they were born has been of particular benefit in limiting the press interest in both Peter and Zara over the years. If they were a Prince and Princess, and were not so far down the line of succession, their every movement might have been closely followed by the media. But people with Royal titles are newsworthy; commoners, even those related to the Queen, are not, unless they are celebrities, as Zara is now finding out. Unlike his sister, Peter remains something of a disappearing Royal to this day. Few people know where he lives or with whom. In fact he shares a house in London with his girlfriend of many years.

When Zara and her brother were at school, their mother was ultra-protective of their privacy. She knew they would be photographed when they were seen in public with her or their grandmother, the Queen, and she reluctantly resigned herself to the fact. However, she drew a distinct line between what she thought were public events and those that she considered to be private. She was furious if reporters and cameramen stepped over the line between the two. The difficulties arose when editors ordered their staff to get stories of human interest that would appeal to their readers. Pictures of Peter Phillips, dressed as a member of his school's fire-fighting team, showing his grandparents, the Queen and the Duke of Edinburgh, around Gordonstoun featured in newspapers throughout the country, and they were very well-received by the public. They were perfectly harmless, and rather endearing. But the Princess Royal was not amused. She felt this was a private occasion and should have been respected as such. However, both the school and the Palace knew in advance what was going to happen, and if either had not wanted the pictures to appear, the photographers could easily have been banned from the private grounds of the school.

The attitude of the Royal Family as a whole to the media is puzzling to say the least. On the one hand they claim to hate an intrusive press, while at the same time they (like Zara) employ press officers to ensure their activities receive favourable coverage. Buckingham Palace has a compact press team, with its staff divided between various members of the family; Prince Philip's press office is said to have the toughest assignment. Every morning the Queen's press secretary presents a digest of the newspaper and magazine coverage of Royal events, underlining those referring to Her Majesty and the Duke of Edinburgh. The Queen will often criticise the press office if something she has attended and that she feels was worth covering does not appear to her to have received sufficient space in the papers. Prince Charles also has a press officer, with the rather grand title of Communications Secretary, who joined Clarence House from Manchester United football club for a salary reported to be in excess of £200,000, nearly four times what the Queen's press secretary is paid.

The Palace press office always returns calls from journalists and they try hard to be cooperative. But they do not show favouritism to any particular organisation or individual. So, even though certain 'Royal watchers' believe they have the inside track, it is really all in the mind. Nobody is given any advantage over his rivals. If a journalist makes personal contact with a member of the Royal Family – and it would only be with one of the juniors – they may get the odd tip off about a story, but it is a rarity rather than the rule.

The Royal Family claim to dislike all photographers. By that they mean press photographers, not family favourites like Lord Snowdon, the Queen's former brother-in-law, or the late Earl of Lichfield. Snowdon, and one or two others on the 'selected' list, is frequently asked to take pictures at various Royal residences. But these are carefully staged affairs with every detail planned well in advance. For large group pictures, such as wedding photographs, the cameramen spend weeks working out where everyone will stand or sit and on the day they will place name cards on the carpet so everyone knows exactly where they should be. For some family pictures the photographers have to use unconventional methods. At one session the Queen wanted the family to be photographed all looking the same way, away from the camera. After much deliberation, placing a television set just out of view of the lens and getting the family to watch a Marx Brothers film obtained the desired result. Her Majesty said later it was one of the most enjoyable photo sessions she had ever experienced. But this friendly, even affectionate attitude to the favoured few does not extend to press photographers in general, but didn't displease her.

Prince Philip is known for his outright hatred of the media, saying as far back as 1954, 'God save us from those bloody vultures,' while Princess Anne, in answer to a press photographer who said he hoped he wasn't being a pest, said, 'You are a pest, by the very nature of that camera in your hand.'

When Peter and Zara were very small they were often taken to Sandringham and Balmoral by their parents. The Queen loved having her first grandchildren by her side whenever she walked in the grounds and she was often seen leading the children on their ponies. The difficulties arose when dozens of photographers and reporters gathered near the stables and began clicking away the moment the Royal party appeared. At Sandringham, a public road runs alongside the stable block, so it is impossible to prevent anyone from standing there unless they are causing an obstruction. Similarly, at Balmoral, public footpaths criss-cross the extensive 50,000-acre grounds, so there is the same problem.

At that age, Zara was not aware of the furore she was inadvertently causing. She thought it was perfectly natural for crowds to gather whenever she appeared. As a child growing up in the bosom of the Royal Family, press attention was as normal to her as the lack of it is to any ordinary child. On one occasion, the Queen was leading Zara around Sandringham when she sensed the cameras were beginning to upset the pony. In what was for her a rare occurrence, she spoke sharply to the assembled photographers and reporters, saying, 'I wish you would go away.' They obeyed, but only after confirming to each other that they had the right quote from Her Majesty. It was another scoop for the Royal watchers.

The first few times Zara made headlines on her own occurred when she had a public brawl with her then-boyfriend Richard

Johnson, and when she was discovered wearing a stud in her tongue and her navel. In another piece of early press coverage, she was voted one of the fifty most beautiful women in the world in a poll, an accolade that amused her greatly.

Like most members of the Royal Family, Zara is not entirely blameless for the press coverage she receives, but in many cases hers is a no-win situation. When she and Richard Johnson sold their story exclusively to *Hello!* magazine for a sum believed to be over £100,000, it was gloves off as far as the rest of the press were concerned. They felt that if she was prepared to accept money to reveal the secrets of her lifestyle, then it was open season, and the tabloids had a field day. Zara knows now it was a mistake to invite *Hello!* into the home she shared with Johnson and reveal personal details of their life together. She has grown up since then and definitely won't repeat the exercise. She has become a very private person and gets embarrassed when she reads comments about her figure. There was even one article that speculated that she was pregnant because the reporter imagined she had put on a few pounds. It wasn't true.

Zara learned the hard way that sometimes you can attract more attention than you bargained for. A month after the *Hello!* piece, she and Richard hit the headlines for all the wrong reasons when it was revealed that they had brawled in the street outside the house of jockey Warren Marston. A witness told the press that Zara was screaming and shouting and that the couple punched and kicked each other over allegations that Zara had flirted with Marston. The witness was the man they had hired for the evening to drive them and a group of friends to a restaurant so they could have a few drinks and not worry about driving themselves. He was a regular driver and they had no reason to suspect that he was about to betray them to the press. But a few days later he sold his story to a Sunday newspaper, with lurid details of the stand-up fight Richard and Zara had had in the street. He then disappeared from the local scene and none of them saw anything of him again. Those who were present at the time of the incident have never spoken publicly about it, so whatever really happened, they are keeping to themselves. That something out-of-the-ordinary took place is fairly obvious, but whether it was as bad as the papers reported is another matter. Regardless, the principal individuals involved are still friends; Richard Johnson, Warren Marston and Zara all still speak to each other, so it cannot have been too serious. Nevertheless, it did not do Zara's image much good, and Buckingham Palace were not pleased (Palace-speak for absolutely furious). Zara made sure there was no chance of a repeat performance.

Two years before this incident it was reported that Zara had thrown a notorious party at the home of her father. It was an Ann Summers sex party, with different kinds of lingerie and sex toys on show. Twenty-five of Zara's girl friends turned up and they were reported to have guzzled champagne and eaten smoked salmon as waiters, clad only in PVC G-strings, moved among them. Mark Phillips was said not to have been present at the time and his reaction to the event has not been revealed. Zara said later that the incident was exaggerated beyond all belief. In the first place, she was not the person who held the party. It was given by a girlfriend of her brother, Peter, and she said she didn't know when she was invited what sort of party it was going to be. There was drink available, as there always is at these affairs, and there was also a lot of laughter and boisterous behaviour. None of the other girls present was named but, of course, Zara being who she is, the party made headlines, with her name prominent in the story. You couldn't blame the press. Someone had tipped them off and it made a brilliant story.

Both Zara and Peter featured in the press from time to time when they were in their late teens. On one occasion, they scandalised watchers when they were spotted at the Gatcombe Horse Trials in 1999 swigging beer from bottles. It wasn't the fact that they were actually drinking alcohol that disgusted those that saw them, but simply that they were not using glasses. Very plebeian and un-royal!

It was at another horse trials, this time the Northampton event in June 2003, that Zara had to call for police help in getting rid of unwelcome attention from the press. She was changing clothes in the back of her horsebox, having inadvertently left the rear doors open. At first she couldn't see anyone about, but then she spotted four photographers lurking behind some trees, all trying to snap her undressing – pictures that would have sold for a small fortune if they had been successful. As the police chased the photographers away, Zara called after them, 'You think you're so clever, but I can see you. Go away!' (or words to that effect). The photographers were not staff photographers from British newspapers, but freelancers or paparazzi, who try to sell their pictures all over the world. If they had managed to catch Zara with her pants down, literally, they would all have made thousands of pounds, but on this occasion they were thwarted. Since then she has always been very careful about where she changes – and who is around at the time.

Zara does not go out of her way to cultivate the press. Indeed, it wasn't until she accepted commercial sponsorship for her equestrian activities that she began to make herself available to the media at all. Now she realises that the companies that pay her lots of money to advertise their products will not continue to do so if they think they are not getting good value. So she is very cooperative at horse shows and other functions where the sponsors want her to meet the press. The only difference now from when she started is that in those days she was quite prepared to be photographed as she was: if it was hot and she was sweaty with a shiny face after a hard competition, so be it. She didn't expect hairdressers and make-up artists to be on hand to make her look her best. These days, she knows her sponsors expect her to be on top form and she puts up cheerfully with all the paraphernalia that entails.

Once Zara started to make her mark as a three day event competitor, the press began to sit up and really take notice. They remembered how her mother had provided them with a fund of stories and pictures 30 years earlier, particularly her 'Naff off' remarks to reporters when they tried to get her to say something worthwhile after she had just completed a tough cross-country course. They needed a new Royal celebrity; there had been a massive gap since the death of Princess Diana in 1997, and they knew that Royals still sold newspapers. So Zara was lined up to fill the vacant role, and she did so brilliantly. She photographed well, was fearless and talented on horseback, and she has since given the press pack the added ingredient of living with two glamorous boyfriends, one a leading National Hunt jockey, the other, a stylish rugby player who was a member of the England World Cup-winning side in 2004. Zara obliged the media and her sponsors by making herself available, or at least, not hiding away whenever someone with a camera appeared. She knew Richard was a celebrity in his own right and when they agreed to sell their story to *Hello!* magazine, it was as much due to him as her. The saccharine taste of the feature did no harm to the Royal Family, apart from the fact that newspapers who had not been given the opportunity to bid for the story had a field day running their own versions of the affair, and then decrying the fact that Zara had let the side down by 'going commercial'. It was all self-righteous humbug, and if the couple had then had the benefit of an experienced agent, they could have negotiated an even larger fee from one of the national newspapers, to whom six-figure sums for celebrity exclusives are commonplace.

What Zara had discovered was that once you become a celebrity, whether it's as a sportsman, athlete, pop star or actor, you become part of the media circus. There's little you can do about it. The 'regular people' who are propelled into the limelight simply by being contestants in reality television shows often discover that suddenly they have become famous – just for being famous. Many of them seem to love the spotlight and wallow in being the focus of attention. With the Royal Family, it is different. They are born into celebrity. If Zara's grandmother did not happen to be Queen, then she obviously would never have received half the attention she subsequently attracted. Even after winning the world title in 2006, the spotlight would have faded had she not been who she is. Who can name the last person before Zara to win the World Three Day Event Championship?

The problem Zara has with the press is that what she would like them to print is never the same as what they want to know. She is willing to talk about horses and her achievements, and when she is interviewed as part of the British team she insists that the other members are present too. It doesn't make any difference; the reporters – apart from the genuine equestrian press – are interested only in her, not in the others. They want to know about her love life, her clothes, whether she likes to shop and what are her favourite drink, food and movie. They want to hear about the partying, the cutting-edge outfits, and still, after all these years, the tongue piercing. She always tries to steer the conversation around to horses and she does her best to be frank and honest with them all. But she becomes disillusioned when the story she has given the press comes out as something completely different from what she has said. Her idea of what constitutes a human-interest story and the newspapers' idea obviously are miles apart. Editors know what their readers demand and as long as they get decent quotes from stars like Zara, they are happy to print accounts that leave out many of the things the interviewees feel are of the most interest . . . and nearly every story that appears – anywhere in the world – will have a reference to the 'Royal Rebel' nickname.

When Zara was selected for the British Equestrian Team for the World Championships, her boss, the team manager Yogi Breisner, issued notes giving advice on how to handle the media. They were not intended solely for Zara, but for everyone, junior and senior alike. The handbook states, 'We do not use mobile phones during any training or team meetings.' This is excellent advice, as reporters have a tendency to ring up at the most inopportune moments, interrupting training or team talks. When Zara was with the team, she was often asked to give interviews to local radio stations over the phone, and she used Yogi's help to determine which interviews to accept. He didn't want to forbid his riders from getting publicity, as it was good for the team as a whole, but by singling out Zara for questions, the reporters were in danger of making her team-mates jealous. After all, at this time she was the most junior team member and by far the youngest. Zara was invariably polite with reporters, but she did get a bit fed up when all they wanted to know was what she was going to wear and if she had any plans to become engaged.

As she has become a well-known face and name on the celebrity circuit, Zara has reached an accommodation with the press. She does not come under the protective umbrella of the Buckingham Palace press office for her media coverage. Instead the Palace refer all callers to Gatcombe, where, in turn, they are directed to her public relations company in London, who filter all applications for interviews, and ensure Zara's press coverage is carefully monitored in order to show her at her best. If an enquiry is about her riding and the PR people are convinced the reporters are genuine, an interview will usually be set up. But with the press eager to grasp at every morsel of juicy news about Zara, the situation did at one stage get to the point where, in order to defend herself, she decided to accept an offer from one of Britain's national newspapers to write a number of columns on equestrianism. Of course, she didn't have to sit down in front of a computer and type the articles herself. It's her unique insight they wanted, so a journalist rang her up and asked questions, which he then put into the form the newspaper wanted. In this way, Zara was able to control, to some extent, the coverage she received, and divert queries away from her 'Royal rebel' image.

One thing that particularly annoys Zara about the media is that on the one hand they use her as tabloid fodder and on the other they criticise the Royal Family for being out of touch with the real, modern world. Her uncle, Prince Charles, is ridiculed as a fuddy-duddy, who talks to his plants and dresses and acts as his father and grandfather did. But when William, Harry and Zara try to live like any other young people of their age, they are not held up as examples of the kind of young Royal who should be accepted as assets to the country and the monarchy.

There is a line to be drawn between what type of press coverage is acceptable to both the Royals and the public, but the difficulty lies in deciding who is going to draw that line. If Zara's alleged transgressions, such as giving Richard Johnson a congratulatory kiss in public after he had won a prestigious race, are the worst sins she has committed in what some people feel is conduct unbecoming for a member of the Royal Family, then we do not have too much to worry about. They do not compare, for example, with the lurid pictures and stories from over a decade ago of the Duchess of York in the South of France, lying topless on a sun bed and having her toes sucked by her 'financial adviser', or the ambitions of the Prince of Wales to be Camilla Parker Bowles' 'tampon', revealed in a telephone conversation between the two. All of these stories can truthfully be said to be private, but millions of people, not only in Britain, but also throughout the world, devoured the acres of newsprint devoted to the accounts. So, if Zara wants to draw a line between *her* public life and what she considers to be private, she would do well to keep her activities out of sight. She cannot have it both ways and neither can the press.

Zara Phillips has, on the whole, received a favourable press and she would be the first to admit it. She knows that to attract commercial sponsors, which she needs if she is to successfully continue her riding career, she must cooperate with the media. They need each other. If the press stopped publishing stories and pictures of her, her sponsors would fall away so fast it would take her breath away. The press also knows that stories and photographs of a glamorous young Royal beauty on a massive horse are always going to increase circulation. They learned that with the late Diana, Princess of Wales (although in her case she was never caught on horseback). Her sons, Princes William and Harry, attract a fair amount of media attention, but until one of them becomes particularly newsworthy for their own actions, Zara will continue to be good value for the press, and will continue to benefit from that attention, at least for the time being.

In the modern world, it is difficult to overestimate the importance of the relations between Royalty and the press: without the media, no one would know anything about the Royal Family. Both sides realise this, and while the press try to emphasise that what they are doing is in the public interest, the Royal Family is only interested in press coverage where they can control it. Prince Harry already knows to his cost that, unlike most of his friends, he cannot get away with anything. In 2001, he was involved in an under-age drinking incident in a pub near Highgrove, where drugs were also being taken (which he was not accused of). The story made headlines around the world, and again more recently Harry made headlines when he was pictured, apparently the worse for wear, leaving a nightclub at 3 a.m. And like Harry, Prince Charles, the late Princess Diana, Princess Margaret, the Duke and Duchess of York, and the Earl and Countess of Wessex, have all discovered that where the media is concerned, there is no such thing as being able to bury the past. It always comes back to haunt you.

It took the Queen many years to understand that she needed to reach an accommodation with the press. She discovered it in a painful manner at the time of the trial of her former footman, Paul Burrell, when she suddenly remembered a conversation they had had some time before, regarding property he was accused of stealing from the late Diana, Princess of Wales. The case against him collapsed as the result of her recollection, and Her Majesty received coverage in the media that was less than favourable. It also took the Queen some time to regain the public's affection after the death of Diana in 1997. The public's initial reaction was anger and disappointment at the way she had behaved and it took all her natural astuteness and knowledge to influence the media and get people back on her side.

Unlike some older members of her family, Zara copes brilliantly with the press. She is outgoing and honest in her opinions, and is guided by professionals who make sure she does not put a foot wrong. Her mother was for years the Royal the press loved to hate – the feeling was said to be mutual – yet even she has reached an understanding with them recently. She still does not go out of her way to help reporters and photographers, but at least she no longer deliberately antagonises those who turn up to cover her events. If she can do it, so can the rest of the Royal Family. Zara is starting with a far greater advantage; the media already regard her as a star.

13 MISS MONEYBAGS

In common with every other member of the Royal Family, Zara dislikes discussing money (even though she is said to be worth over £3 million) and like all the others, she is always pleading poverty. All the Royals, from the Queen down, are forever saying they cannot afford to buy such and such an item, while living in the lap of luxury and eating and drinking the best that money can buy. Why they should like to pretend that they are living on the breadline when everyone knows there is nothing they cannot afford is one of life's great mysteries.

Unlike many other members of her family, and contrary to what many misinformed people believe, Zara is not on the Civil List, so she does not receive any money from the public purse. Nor does she receive an allowance from the Queen or the Princess Royal. In fact, it was only after securing sponsorship contracts that Zara was able to truly excel in the incredibly expensive world of three day eventing.

It was in February 2003 (three years before she secured her world title) that Zara became the first member of the Royal Family to sign a commercial sponsorship deal when she agreed to become the public face of betting firm Cantor Index. It meant she would be wearing the company's logo discreetly on her riding gear whenever she competed, and she would also make herself available at horse trials throughout the country, meeting and greeting Cantor Index's important clients.

When the deal was announced, one of the company's partners, James Blackshaw, revealed that instead of him seeking Zara out, the initiative came from her. They had met at Cheltenham Races and she had asked if his company would like to sponsor her after he had asked her to sponsor him running in the London marathon. At the time he wasn't too sure what she did and when she replied 'Everything', he had to do some homework before he agreed to her proposal. She offered him £5 if he completed the marathon, but it took some months before she coughed up the money.

James Blackshaw and Cantor Index, now part of financial brokers BGC Partners, are delighted with the results of their sponsorship of Zara. Mr Blackshaw said that once Zara realised she was being paid to do a job, she knew she had to take it seriously and perform, and she did. In the first year of the sponsorship she came second at Burleigh, then won the European Championship followed by the World title, so both sides of the deal got value for money. Zara was paid £30,000 by Cantor during the first year of their partnership and she said that although it was a tremendous help, it only covered her stable expenses for things like food for the horses and vets' bills. She was praised for her initiative in getting the sponsorship, but she was also realistic enough to realise that it had as much to do with her Royal status as her talent as a rider in those days.

Of course, Zara has all of the attributes any worthwhile sponsor could ask for. She is attractive, accessible, articulate – unless she is making an acceptance speech at an awards ceremony – and has one quality every other celebrity in the world would kill for: she is Royal, and that is something even money cannot buy.

If there is one aspect of the monarchy that is guaranteed to arouse envy and anger in the populace, it is the amount of money the Royal Family possesses and their apparent greed in keeping it to themselves. Prince Charles's extravagant lifestyle and the vast sums he spends on himself and Camilla attracts particular attention, and appals even some of the other members of his family, though none would ever allow a word of criticism to be voiced in their presence. It has been said that the Prince thinks nothing of sending a servant on a 200-mile round trip because he has forgotten to pack a pair of the Prince's favourite cuff links. Charles and the Duchess of Cornwall live in Clarence House with nearly one hundred staff to look after two people, and also own a large estate in Gloucestershire and the handsome Birkhall in Scotland, which Charles inherited from his grandmother, Queen Elizabeth, and on which he has spent £2 million bringing it up to his exacting standards. Charles has also spent another million buying a farmhouse in Carmarthenshire in Wales so that he can, at last, truthfully claim he has a home in the Principality from which he takes his title. So, four homes, plus Camilla's £3 million Raymill House in Wiltshire, just a few miles from Highgrove, which she kept after she married Charles so that she could have a 'bolthole' to retreat to when things get a little too much for her. And when the Queen squandered £5 million (of her own money it must be admitted) in building 'Southyork', the appalling architectural monstrosity in Windsor Great Park, for Prince Andrew and Sarah Ferguson to share when they were married – and in which they lived for less than five years – it was seen as the unacceptable face of ostentatious wealth being flaunted in the face of the people of the United Kingdom.

The situation of Zara's parents is somewhat different. Her father, Mark Phillips, has no money of his own, apart from what he earns, as he wasn't left any great fortune by his parents. Her mother, the Princess Royal, relies almost entirely on her allowance from the Civil List, which pays the expenses for her public duties and also the administrative costs of running her small office at Buckingham Palace.

There has always been confusion over the true wealth of the Windsors. The Queen used to be described as the richest woman in the world, with an estimated fortune of around

£100 million, but even with that sum, she would be far down the list of the world's richest people today. Oil-rich Arab sheiks, Russian industrial tycoons and American computer billionaires all make Her Majesty's money look like small change in comparison. However, no one disputes that by any standards the House of Windsor is among the wealthiest in Britain, even if much of the fortune, if you count the Royal art collection, is held in trust for the nation. Enough remains in the family's private collection of fabulous jewels, diamonds, priceless works of art, furniture, strings of racehorses, and a huge property portfolio, not to mention their investments in business enterprises, where the Queen and her family are advised by some of the country's leading financial minds, to place them securely near the top of the British rich list.

If the Royal Family is accused of being parsimonious, the reply is always the same. They point out that what others might regard as meanness is, in fact, just good old solid, Hanoverian housekeeping and frugality. They do not like talking about their money, regarding the subject as vulgar, but when, for example, one of them needs to lease a car, as the Princess Royal does with her Bentley, they do become involved in the negotiations, although at a safe distance. Her Royal Highness pays nearly £3,000 a month for her vehicle, but as she uses it mostly for official business, the cost comes out of the Civil List, not her own pocket. It's just as well, as the new price for the vehicle is around £180,000.

Apart from members of the family themselves, only one person in the world knows the true extent of each of their fortunes. It is not a banker (the Royal Family banks at Coutts, now a branch of National Westminster), neither is it the Royal stockbroker or even the Lord Chamberlain, head of the Royal Household. It is the Keeper of the Privy Purse – and, yes, there is such an object. It is a silk purse about eighteen inches square, in which the Keeper used to place gold coins for the sovereign to disburse to deserving cases when he walked among his subjects. These days, the Keeper of the Privy Purse is better known among his colleagues as the man in charge of the Royal chequebook. He is the man who knows all the Royal Family's financial secrets, and is telling none of them. If he were to write a book, he could increase his own bank account by several millions. When members of the Royal Family need to buy anything, the Keeper knows, without being told, that he has to negotiate massive discounts, and not pay the bill until the final demand has arrived. The late Princess Margaret once boasted that she had never paid the full retail price for anything in her life, and the same can be said for current members of the family.

The Queen and her family believe in the 'need to know' principle, so they divide their wealth into segments that are kept separate from all the others, and only those involved with each segment is privy to the secret of that particular amount. So the bank may know how many cheques flow into and out of the Royal accounts, but they do not know if theirs is the only account, as some of the Royal Family's banking business is conducted in nominee names. It is a system that has worked remarkably well for generations, and as the Queen's family has expanded, with marriage and grandchildren being born, the need for discretion has become more and more important.

One rule the Queen has insisted upon for all her family is that no one is allowed to keep money in offshore accounts and neither are they permitted to own property outside the United Kingdom. Stories claiming that Her Majesty owned blocks of apartments in New York were denied when Buckingham Palace issued a formal statement.

The immediate result of Zara winning the World Championships was that a flood of offers came pouring in for her to endorse various products, with fees starting at over £100,000. Celebrities of any kind – sporting, film, pop and even reality TV show – find that the gates of commercial exploitation open wide for them as soon as they achieve fame (or infamy) and they are suddenly showered with more money than they can count.

Zara's Australian agent, a keen negotiator who handles the affairs of a number of famous sports personalities and television stars, as well as Zara's father, for whom he has worked for 30 years, realised straightaway the value of having a client who was not only a World Champion, but a good-looking Royal to boot. He organised several lucrative contracts for his client in the aftermath of her victory in Germany and she quickly accepted sponsorship deals with Land Rover and Rolex, two of the most prestigious and upmarket products in the world. Inevitably, Zara's acceptance of sponsorship attracted criticism from some quarters, not because she was Royal, but because she was allowing her name to be associated with Land Rover, a company accused by the Campaign Against the Arms Trade of selling its vehicles to countries that used them to suppress peaceful protests. The CAAT issued a statement saying, 'We're very disappointed that a public figure such as Zara Phillips would choose to endorse Land Rover. It's an unethical company which sells equipment to oppressive regimes.'

There is no hard evidence that a single person rushed out and bought either a Land Rover or a £5,000 Rolex watch just because they saw Zara promoting them, unlike products endorsed by, say, David Beckham, whose sponsors claim that products advertised by him show an immediate increase in sales. But Zara's endorsement, in full-page newspaper and magazine advertisements, keeps the names of her companies in the minds of potential customers, and that is of course the general idea of advertising and celebrity endorsement. It is an association of images of her, a winning equestrian, with the companies' products, which makes them winners also in the eyes of the consumer. Zara could cash in on her success by franchising out various parts of her riding outfits to different sports companies. The big names such as Nike and Adidas would be delighted to see their names on her sweaters or riding hats. Six-figure sums are hers for the asking if she wants to turn herself into a walking, or in her case, riding advertising hoarding. Tennis players and world-class golfers are all sponsored in this way. The television companies know it and raise no objections. When Michael Schumacher won his several Formula One world titles, he always appeared at the press conference afterwards sporting a cap bearing the logo of one of his main advertisers. Zara hasn't yet got to that stage, and she would need the approval of the FEI (the International Federation for Equestrian Sports) before she could accept such endorsements. At the moment, the deals she does have are working brilliantly for all concerned.

Zara would not have accepted any sponsorship deal without the approval of both her mother and the Queen, and when she was asked how Her Majesty felt about her first steps into commercialisation, she replied, 'I want to stand on my own two feet. Apart from wanting to achieve things in my own right, I think my grandmother has quite enough to worry about before she gets to me.'

Zara has recently added another backer to her portfolio of sponsors by becoming a global ambassador for the Royal Bank of Scotland – the company that also happens to employ her brother Peter. There's nothing like keeping it in the family.

Both Zara and Mark Phillips give good value for the money they are paid by the sponsors. At the Gatcombe Horse Trials, Mark talks visitors through the cross-country course he has designed, accompanied by his daughter, who makes remarks about the complexity of the course and how one obstacle is so much more difficult than the next. While Mark's remarks are fairly technical, Zara realises that she should not attempt to talk over the heads of non-equestrian guests, and she spices her conversation with little bits of harmless gossip about other celebrities – but not the Royal Family, which is what the guests would really love to hear about. The sponsors' VIP guests will have been given a good lunch and lots of champagne by the time of the tour, so they are in a receptive mood. They cannot believe how informal Zara is, laughing and chatting to all and sundry. She is not in the least bit affected, and she has the ability to remember their names once they have been introduced, which they find very flattering. As they gather in the BGC (the sponsors) tent, Zara works the canvas room. She has inherited one trait at least from the Princess Royal, in that when she is talking to one person, she concentrates totally on that man or woman, and does not look over their shoulder to see if there is anyone more interesting in the room. When they leave, they take with them the impression that she has been genuinely pleased to meet them. Everyone is happy: sponsors, guests and paid celebrity.

Zara's agent told me that she needed sponsorship contracts because she does not receive an allowance from her mother, or from the Queen. In other words, she has no income and she has to be self-supporting. What he failed to mention is that she is the beneficiary of a large trust fund set up for her by the Queen on the day of her birth in 1981, and still administered on her behalf. What it is worth today is anybody's guess. The trust is administered by three trustees, appointed by the Queen and the Princess Royal. They are the Prince of Wales, Andrew Parker Bowles and Sir Jackie Stewart. These last two take most of the decisions regarding Zara's finances, but the Prince of Wales is always consulted before any major policies are decided upon. Sir Jackie, one of the Princess Royal's oldest friends (his wife Helen is Zara's Godmother) is an astute businessman as well as a former World Champion Formula One racing driver, and he is said to have a brilliant financial brain. The trustees have only one common aim: to obtain the best results for the beneficiary of the trust, Zara. They guard her interests with fierce determination. If she wants something that they feel is not in her best interests, they will refuse to allow her to draw from the fund. At the same time, they realise that she needs certain amounts of money to sustain her career and way of life, and they are sympathetic when she makes an approach, but she has to make a good case before they part with any of her money. She may become angry if she feels they are being unreasonable, but she knows deep down that they only have her best interests at heart. She won't have complete control over the money until she is thirty, and until then a tight rein is kept on her funds. As a horsewoman, Zara knows all about tight reins.

When the Queen established the trust fund for Zara, it was set up with £1 million. The trustees make her an allowance, believed to be around £15,000 a year, for her personal expenses, and she was also left money by her great-grandmother, Queen Elizabeth, the Queen Mother. A conservative estimate of the total of Zara's worth today would be in excess of £3 million, but it is all tied up in her trust fund.

Nobody would suggest that Zara is in the same league financially as her cousins, Princes William and Harry, who not only have trust funds of their own, but who also benefited greatly as the sole heirs to their mother's £17 million fortune (most of it accumulated during the divorce settlement from Prince Charles) when she died in 1997. They will never have to worry about paying the gas or electric bill. But realistically, neither will Zara. Her parents paid for her education at school and university, and for all her overseas travel arrangements during her gap year. She has run her own car since passing her test and she always pays her share when out dining and drinking with her friends. Before she was lucky enough to secure her present contracts, with their six-figure payments, she still had to pay her stable fees and the wages of her grooms. So, if there was no allowance from anywhere, where did the money come from? If Zara was so badly off before she received her first lucrative contracts, how is it that she was able to maintain several horses, including stabling costs, vets' bills and the use of the yard at Gatcombe, for which, it is said, she pays her mother rent? As a private individual, it is, of course, entirely her own business, but as a member of the Royal Family, it is not too surprising that there is speculation about the extent and source of her fortune.

If the Queen does give her granddaughter any financial help, it is of course entirely a private matter, nobody's business but those involved, and the public will never know about it. But obviously the money to pay for Zara's sporting costs in the days before her sponsorship deals had to come from somewhere, but where? The simple answer is that, while she may not have had an official monthly allowance from her parents, they met all her expenses, with a little help from a generous grandmother. So money has never been a major problem.

Even so, given the great expense of her chosen profession and the relative lack of significant private funds available to her, Zara has been forced to do what many other sportsmen and women do: she set out to finance herself by obtaining commercial sponsorship. And it was only after securing her first contract and being able to run her own stable that success in horse trials started to come. She was finally ready to make her mark. The more recent sponsorship that becoming World Champion has attracted has relieved her parents of the financial obligation of providing for their daughter, and she is now able to stand on her own two feet.

In common with every other celebrity, Zara does not reveal the amounts she receives from her commercial activities, but an educated guess puts the sum for each of her sponsorship deals well into six figures. So with annual running costs for her equestrian pursuits amounting to nearly half a million pounds, Zara's advertising revenue, less her agent's commission of course, is probably worth over three-quarters of that amount. Her finances have now been put on a proper business footing and she has formed a limited company, registered for Value Added Tax. This means the 17.5 per cent VAT she is charged on purchases can be claimed back, as is the case for all businesses.

Her accounts are kept in immaculate order; bills are paid promptly and discounts negotiated ruthlessly. There's nothing underhand about this, it is just sound business practice. Buckingham Palace does it for the Queen, and Prince Charles's Private Secretary, Sir Michael Peat, a former Keeper of the Privy Purse to the Queen, and also one of the City's most astute financial brains, advises his master on the most efficient methods of keeping costs down and maximising profits at the Duchy of Cornwall, the organisation that provides the Prince of Wales with his income.

If Zara is chosen to represent Great Britain in the 2008 Olympic Games, her price will go through the roof. And if she manages to add the Olympic crown to her world title, she will be able to write her own cheque. The world's leading sports manufacturers have millions to spend on celebrity advertising and they are just waiting to throw buckets of it at her.

Even though Zara is eleventh in the line of succession to the throne, she does not undertake public engagements on behalf of the Queen, and neither does she stand in for her mother on public occasions. The Queen would welcome her granddaughter's presence at certain Royal functions, but she accepts the Princess Royal's decision not to allow Zara to take a role in the family firm at the moment. As we know, Princess Anne deliberately declined the Queen's offer of titles for both Peter and Zara when they were born as she knew that eventually they would move so far down the succession that there was virtually no chance they would ever become King or Queen, and so they would have to make a living of their own. That is why, when Zara became the first Royal to appear in a paid advertisement in a national newspaper, the *Mail on Sunday*, on 9 December 2006, Buckingham Palace said that while they had not had any advance notice that she was going to appear, 'How she runs her career is her own affair.'

The advertisement for Land Rover was brilliantly photographed by Mary McCartney, daughter of former Beatle, Sir Paul, at a former home of Sir Winston Churchill, the Templeton Estate at Roehampton in Surrey. It was no mere coincidence that the setting could easily have been mistaken for one of the rooms in Buckingham Palace.

In agreeing to accept substantial fees for appearing in these advertisements, Zara knew she would be in line for criticism from some quarters. But she was pleasantly surprised at the comments of the Labour Member of Parliament for Glasgow East, who welcomed her foray into the commercial world, saying, 'Miss Phillips is to be commended for making her own way in the world. If she's cashing in on her success as a sporting star as other people do, then she is making something of herself.'

Zara's brother, Peter, is also trying to make his way by working as a hospitality manager in Formula One racing, a job that he obtained with the help of Sir Jackie Stewart. Peter is quite happy being out of the limelight and doing something he loves. It was the legendary Sir Jackie who first introduced Peter to motor racing, opening many doors, and Peter now earns a modest but comfortable living out of what was once a hobby and is now a full-time occupation.

The Queen is delighted that two of her grandchildren are standing on their own feet. The fact that neither undertakes public duties and that they do not have the disadvantage of a title to weigh them down means that they are expected to pay their own way and cannot be accused of being Royal hangers-on, or of cashing in on their connections. This, of course, was the reason why the Queen's daughter-in-law, the Countess of Wessex, was forced to relinquish her public relations firm's lucrative contract with Rover, for which the company was paid £250,000.

Whatever Zara does to raise money to fund her sporting pursuits, she cannot win. There will always be some people who will say she is just another minor Royal trading on her family connections to make a fortune, and that without those connections, no business would want to know her. If, on the other hand, she sat back and did nothing for herself and persuaded her grandmother to fund her sporting activities, which, no doubt, would be possible and highly probable if Her Majesty thought Zara needed it, then many people would regard her as nothing but a parasite, playing at her sport but not pursuing it as a full-time professional.

Of course, Zara is not the first member of her immediate (non-Royal) family to accept money from commercial sponsors. As far back as the 1970s, Mark Phillips secured a contract with Land Rover to advertise their vehicles and he also made television commercials in Australia and New Zealand, but not, out of respect for the Queen, in Britain. And on 6 August 1983, Princess Anne and her husband made history by allowing the grounds of their home to open to the paying public for the first time, when they organised the first Gatcombe Horse Trials under the auspices of the Croft Original wine company. The grounds were open but there was strict security to prevent anyone getting anywhere near the house itself.

The Princess Royal and her former husband continue to organise shooting days at Gatcombe, to which parties of sportsmen and women are invited, for a fee. These occasions are thoroughly professional, and profitable, and the money goes into the company owned by the estate. There is nothing wrong with this; it is a perfectly legitimate business operation and the accounts are available for inspection when required. The estate at Gatcombe has to pay for itself. It is too large, at nearly 1,000 acres (more if you include Aston Farm) to be run purely as a home for the daughter of the Queen.

Zara is a realist when it comes to money. She acknowledges that she will never starve or be short of the odd pound or two. She also knows that compared to other young women of her age, she is in a very privileged position. But she wants to be able to contribute to the running costs of her stable of three day event horses. If she is to remain a world-beater, she must have the best facilities available to keep on level terms with her rivals, and that means spending money and lots of it.

In three day eventing, money can flow out like water. It never seems to be coming in. Zara, for example, does not have the problem that faced by her team-mate at the World Championships, Daisy Dick. Daisy was in her horsebox in traffic on a day when high winds forced a large chestnut tree to topple over. She couldn't move as the car in front had stalled, so she simply had to watch as the tree crashed onto her horsebox, practically destroying it. Luckily, she had the foresight to jump out of the front seat and into the back so she wasn't injured, but it meant she had to borrow a truck from friends in order to get to training sessions. She managed to get her own vehicle repaired, but it took some weeks and cost a small fortune. Now, if that happened to Zara, someone – her mother or grandmother – would be able to provide a replacement immediately. The cost wouldn't come into it. That is one area where Zara doesn't have to concern herself too much with money. This doesn't mean she is frivolous about her finances, far from it, but it obviously helps to come from a family for whom the cost of the next horsebox is not a problem.

The three day event teams of the United States, Germany and Australia appear to have unlimited funds to finance their riders and horses. Their facilities are among the finest in the world and they can afford to buy the best horses and hire the best coaches around, hence Mark Phillips' contract with the Americans. No one in Britain could afford to pay him what the Americans pay. But he has to come up with the goods. Results are what matters, as in all sports, and if a national team does not win medals in international competition, the coach is sent packing. As Mark has been with the US team for fifteen years, he must be doing something right, and he is well on target for the 2008 Olympic Games, where his team is aiming to win individual as well as team medals. The Great Britain team does not enjoy the same advantages, but the fact that they still manage to win more than their fair share of titles means that attitude and application still count for something.

Whoever wins the medals in 2008 can guarantee that the coach will be paid a huge bonus, and the winning riders will be the target of offers from every major sports manufacturer in the world. These days, winning is all about money and a gold medal at the Olympic Games is reflected in the amount of cash showered on the victor. Zara's sponsors are hoping that their investment, which has already paid handsome dividends, will next year hit the jackpot.

14 PUBLIC DUTIES AND CHARITIES

As a young, glamorous and photogenic member of the Royal Family with a high profile and sporting success, Zara has been approached many times to perform various duties for charity. Before she accepts any engagement or position, she discusses the proposal with her mother and also, if the engagement warrants it, with her grandmother, the Queen.

The Princess Royal is associated with over five hundred organisations, both civil and military, while the number of the Queen's charities also runs into hundreds. The problem occurs when an organisation, however worthy it may appear, wants a Royal name on its masthead simply to cash in. Few people can resist the opportunity of being linked to a charity if they believe that by doing so they are in the company of a member of the Royal Family.

The Royals all ask the same questions when they are approached to become Patron or President of a particular organisation: why do you want me and what can I do for you if I agree? Zara has a wonderful example to follow in her mother. The Princess Royal takes an active interest in every group she is associated with, attending their meetings when she can and lending her support to their fund-raising events.

She says she has no interest in being a Patron of something simply to allow her name on their headed writing paper. She researches the society or charity thoroughly and her office at Buckingham Palace keeps her informed of all their activities for months before she agrees to join them. And for every twenty invitations she receives to join an organisation, she probably accepts only one or two. She has been President of Save the Children for more than twenty years and she has travelled to every country in the world where the organisation has operations. Riding for the Disabled is another of her pet charities, something she adopted when she was still an active competitor. If anyone asks her if they can make a donation in her name to Riding for the Disabled, she directs them towards a company making specially adapted rocking horses that are ideal for disabled people to use in safety.

Over the years Zara has accompanied her mother to many events for charity, so she has learned what is required when a member of the Royal Family, even one without a title, becomes identified with a particular cause. She has continued her family's long patronage of Great Ormond Street Hospital for Children and has visited the wards on many occasions, especially around Christmas. Most of her visits go unreported and that's the way she prefers it. She is not there for personal publicity, but she knows that a visit from a well-known personality, Royal or not, gives a huge lift to the morale of the patients and staff.

Although the number of charities Zara is associated with does not compare with those of other, more senior members of the Royal Family, and hers are limited mainly to causes close to her heart and about which she has some knowledge, she does throw herself enthusiastically behind them when they ask for her support. The charities she works with are mainly concerned with the equestrian world, spinal injuries and children's causes. No doubt, as she becomes older, the list will grow and expand to include many other interests.

Zara was particularly moved by the plight of those who had suffered in the tsunami disaster in Indonesia on Boxing Day 2005, and she agreed to donate one of her spectacular evening gowns (which she had worn at the London premiere of the film *Seabiscuit*) to be auctioned in aid of the relief fund. It raised several thousand pounds. The successful bidder later said he would have doubled his offer if she had modelled the gown for him personally. If Zara had heard about this unique promise a little earlier she might well have been tempted to take him up on his generous offer.

It was in that same year that Zara agreed to become International Patron of CatWalk, a charity founded to support research into curing spinal injuries. Naturally this is a cause near to Zara's heart as she has seen at first hand the devastating effect an injury to the spine can have in her own sport. Catriona Williams, who founded CatWalk, was a successful three day event competitor until a tragic fall cut short her riding career. She suffered an appalling injury in the fall and was left a tetraplegic. Zara didn't hesitate when she was approached to support the charity, saying she was touched by Catriona's commitment and hoped she could do something to help and bring more awareness to CatWalk's cause. Catriona plays an active part in promoting the work of CatWalk and she says that when she first approached her friends from the world of three day eventing in New Zealand, where she lives, 'Everyone put up their hand to help without question. It was overwhelming.'

The ultimate aim of CatWalk is to find a cure for spinal injuries. The charity tries to make its events fun, but there is always a serious purpose behind them. Zara attended a dinner in aid of the charity in New Zealand in June 2005 and her presence helped to make it a sell-out event, raising a record NZ$400,000 in a single evening. One of the most profitable parts of the evening was an auction where celebrities offered themselves as workers to the highest bidders. Zara went for $25,000 and her 'forfeit' was to work a full shift in a bakery just outside Auckland. She duly completed her task and the money went towards the spinal injury research fund.

Two of the other charities with which Zara is associated are INSPIRE, a charity based in Salisbury that is aimed at improving the quality of life of those people who have been paralysed through spinal cord injuries. INSPIRE is a medical research organisation entirely funded by voluntary contributions. Their objective is to promote the research and development of electronic, mechanical and medical aids to assist and increase the mobility of people confined to wheelchairs or bed. There are some seven hundred spinal cord injuries in Britain every year. Some are caused by riding or other sports, but the majority come about through accidents involving motorbikes and cars, or even falls in the home. The charity was founded in 1985 by people who themselves suffered some sort of spinal injury and who wanted to try and raise money for further research into the causes, and possible cures. INSPIRE has found many unusual ways of raising money, one of which is their annual polo match at Tidworth Polo Club between teams of National Hunt jockeys and three day eventers. An added attraction is a champagne reception followed by lunch with the celebrities after the match. If Zara and her boyfriend, Mike Tindall, make an appearance, even if they don't play, it practically guarantees increased sponsorship and raises the profile of the charity into the bargain.

The United Kingdom's leading children's cancer charity is CLIC Sargent, named after the famous classical music conductor, Sir Malcolm Sargent, and Zara also lends her support to this cause whenever she is asked. The appearance by a member of the Royal Family who is also in the news because of her sporting achievements is a great boost to a fund-raising event, as another of her favourite charities, The Cauldwell Charitable Trust, discovers whenever Zara turns up to one of their functions. The Trust was set up to help children with special needs, disabilities and serious illnesses. They arrange special treats for particularly deserving cases, such as taking children to Lapland to meet Father Christmas, and if the Trust discovers that a dying child has a particular wish, they make sure that wish is granted. They also give money directly to those caring for children and make substantial donations to the NSPCC.

Zara likes everything to do with horses, from pony club events to the Horse of the Year Show, and is always happy to assist organisations that support horse-related pursuits. She enjoys racing, but only as a spectator, and at the time of writing she has not been tempted to follow her mother's example and become a competitive jockey, though she has entered a few charity races. She did, however, become, for a time, the head of Cheltenham's 16–24 Club, an organisation founded to encourage more young people to go racing. The appointment was approved by her mother, who had also consulted the Queen. Her ex-boyfriend, Richard Johnson, said she made a significant contribution by taking on this job, as she is exactly the kind of role model the sport needs if it is to attract a younger generation of race-goer. Being associated with a Royal who also happens to be good-looking was a bonus for Cheltenham, and Zara attended meetings whenever she was asked.

That is one of the nicest things about Zara – when she takes something on, she throws herself in, heart and soul. There are no half measures. Her social skills are excellent and when she goes racing, she enjoys meeting people from all walks of life and of all ages and class. She loves the excitement of racing and the boundless enthusiasm of those who follow the sport. So, would she be tempted to follow in the footsteps of her mother and become a jockey? She says the required level of fitness is now so high and quite honestly she prefers her horses to go a little slower. But no one would be too surprised if it happened sometime in the future. The charity races may have tempted her.

In another charity event, in September 2006, Zara joined a number of other celebrities for a day working at fund-raising on the trading floor of BGC, one of her sponsors. They were trying to raise money to help get children who live in conflict-affected areas of the world back to school. It was a successful day and Zara was glad to be able to make a contribution to this cause.

With the World Championships in 2006, a full programme of events in 2007 and the Olympic Games in 2008, there are massive calls on Zara's time. But if she is able, she tries very hard to accommodate all of her charities and so far none has been refused when they have asked her to make an appearance on their behalf.

At the time of writing, Zara is not a fully-fledged member of 'The Firm', those Royals who regularly undertake public engagements. These are limited to the Queen, the Duke of Edinburgh, the Prince of Wales, the Duke of York, the Earl and Countess of Wessex, the Princess Royal, the Duke and Duchess of Gloucester, the Duke of Kent, Princess Alexandra and the most recent addition, the Duchess of Cornwall. None of Zara's cousins – William, Harry, Beatrice, Eugenie or Louise – have started undertaking regular public duties as yet, William and Harry because of their military commitments, Beatrice, Eugenie and Louise because they are considered too young (although Princess Anne was only eighteen when she began her long career as a full-time Royal).

Contrary to what many people believe, there is no 'clearing house' inside Buckingham Palace. If one member of the Royal Family is asked to perform a particular task and is either unable or unwilling to take it on, they do not pass it on to someone else. As a senior courtier explained, 'We are not in the business of "Rent-a-Royal".'

Zara did, however, receive a rather gentle induction into the public engagement game when she and her mother carried out dual ceremonies to name two ships at the same time. They officially named P&O's *Oceana* and *Adonia*, two new luxury 77,000-tonne cruise liners, at Southampton Docks on 21 May 2005. Professionals choreographed the ceremony, and the one-hour show included an ice dancing spectacular followed by a stunning fireworks display, organised by the man who masterminded the Queen's Golden Jubilee fireworks. The ships were moored bow to bow and Zara and her mother swung their regulation champagne bottles in perfect unison through a ceremonial arc as the Bishop of Southampton blessed the ships with holy water.

Guests said later that Zara carried out her part as if she had been doing it all her life. There was no sign of any nerves and the only person who was even slightly apprehensive on her behalf was the Princess Royal; a natural reaction when your only daughter is performing her first Royal duty under the watchful gaze of television cameras, hundreds of spectators and dozens of press photographers. The Queen Mother used to tell the story of her own first ship launching. Nobody had given her the slightest idea of what to expect and it took her three attempts before the bottle of champagne broke over the bow of the ship, causing her acute embarrassment. It was some years before she was able to see the funny side.

The problem young Royals normally encounter when they are introduced to the never-ending and occasionally stultifying and boring round of opening shops, visiting factories or christening ships, is that there is no one to tell them how to do it. There is no finishing school where they can be instructed in the art of making small talk with people they don't know, have never met before and will never meet again. Princess Anne once told me that she learned the hard way by keeping her eyes open. 'I learned in exactly the same way as a monkey does,' she said. 'By watching your mother and then doing whatever she does.'

The most high-profile appearance that Zara has undertaken to date was a private, yet totally public ceremony. It was the funeral of her great-grandmother, Queen Elizabeth, the Queen Mother, in 2002. One of the largest gatherings of Royalty, religious leaders and politicians in recent memory filled Westminster Abbey, turning the church into a sea of black. Altogether some 2,300 mourners were present with no fewer than thirty-five immediate members of the British Royal Family, who were joined by many European Royals, most of them descendants of Queen Victoria.

Nine senior members of the Royal Family walked behind the cortége, including the Duke of Edinburgh, the Prince of Wales, Prince William and Prince Harry. Zara Phillips accompanied her stepfather, Tim Laurence, in his ceremonial Royal Navy uniform, while Mark Phillips sat in the pews apart from the Royal party. Zara, like all the other Royal ladies, was clad from head to toe in funereal black. It was a solemn occasion and the younger Royal cousins all behaved impeccably. This was one Royal event at which Zara and her family had little to do except be there; everything had been organised down to the tiniest detail years before.

When Zara finally takes her place in the Royal line-up, there will likely be no problems like those experienced by her great-grandmother at her first ship launching, and she will have an easier introduction than her mother. In the first place, she is no longer a teenager, as Princess Anne was when she started taking on public duties, and as a woman nearing her thirties, the confidence is already there. Secondly, Zara has had the examples of both her mother and the Queen to follow. They both carry out their public engagements with flawless professionalism, so Zara could not have better role models. Finally there is already a groundswell of public admiration and affection for her because of her sporting successes and because she has shown she can handle the publicity with grace, good humour and dignity.

At the present time, any thoughts of Zara taking on a larger share of public duties must be relegated far down the list of priorities. She has more than enough to keep her fully occupied with her equestrian ambitions, and anything that interferes with those must take second place. If the Queen asked her to join 'The Firm', Zara would gladly do so, as she cannot refuse her grandmother anything. But Her Majesty is equally anxious for Zara to continue with her riding at an international level and she wouldn't dream of asking her to give up her three day eventing so early in her career. There is so much still for Zara to achieve and when the time comes that she is able to play her part in helping Granny, it will not be necessary to ask her twice.

15 RELAXING

P rincess Anne once told me that she saw no point in going
on holiday if all there was to do was lie on a beach all day.
Similarly, when one of the Queen's Ladies-in-Waiting told
Her Majesty that she had just returned from Barbados and
had spent £5,000 on her holiday, the Queen thought she had
gone mad (a) for going to such a hot climate and (b) for
spending so much money on such a frivolous trip.

Strangely enough, the Court Circular, which lists the
movements of several of the younger members of the Royal
Family as they go about their official business, often shows
that by a strange coincidence they all appear to have to visit
warm climates, such as the Caribbean, in the winter months.
Obviously not all members of the family share the feelings of
the Queen and the Princess Royal about beach holidays!

Zara, unlike her mother and grandmother, is a sun worship-
per. When she was in Australia during her gap year, she
thoroughly enjoyed the pleasures of surfing and swimming
at the magnificent beaches. She says her ideal holiday would
be to charter a yacht and sail around the world with a group
of her closest friends, stopping off wherever they wanted in
small out-of-the-way islands, away from the usual tourist
traps.

The best holiday she has enjoyed to date is one she took with Mike Tindall to Harbour Island in the Bahamas. The couple did their research before they went, looking into the top ten beaches in the world. The one they finally decided upon, Pink Sands beach, was all it promised to be, and they stayed at the Pink Sand Resort, which was the ultimate in luxury and where nobody bothered them. There were acres of space, so privacy was not a problem, and in the evening they could relax with a quiet dinner and excellent wines without having to worry about driving home afterwards. Neither Zara nor Mike like crowded places, so the Bahamas gave them exactly what they were looking for. It was expensive, but they can afford it, so that wasn't a problem. In the future the couple would like to visit Egypt and see the Pyramids. Mike also loves swimming and he wants to do some deep-sea diving, but everything depends on their commitments.

Like many young couples, both Mike and Zara always take their iPods with them on holiday so they can listen to their favourite music, and Mike insists on taking his laptop, so that he can check on his e-mails. He also enjoys reading; Zara is not a great one for books, unless they are about horses. Her idea of a perfect holiday is one where she can chill out and forget everyday chores.

Zara and Mike don't need anyone else with them when they go on holiday and prefer to be left to themselves. It's not that they are anti-social, and when they do meet other holiday-makers they are friendly enough. But in Britain their lives are lived in something of a goldfish bowl, so solitude is a blessing when they are abroad. They both agree that they enjoy luxury: travelling first class, drinking champagne and staying in five-star hotels. Neither is likely to be seen back-packing around the world, staying in youth hostels or camping out under stars.

Mike, who usually does the packing for the couple (he's had plenty of practice with his many overseas tours playing rugby, and he reckons he can cram everything into one suitcase), makes lists before they go away. He remembers with dread the day he forgot to pack his passport, so now that is his number one priority. Zara travels light: several T-shirts, a few pairs of shorts and swimsuits, and at least one decent dress in case they decide to go out to a nice restaurant for a meal. Zara enjoys travelling, even the bit about getting to the airport and the flying. Long-haul flights don't bother her; she doesn't worry too much about jetlag, but they do get a certain amount of VIP treatment when they arrive at the airport. Even if they have booked economy, they are often upgraded to business class and offered the use of the airline's special lounge. Mike hates the actual travelling, but loves arriving in a new place.

As a young girl, Zara was forced to endure the dubious pleasures of holidays at Balmoral in the summer months. Balmoral was bought by Queen Victoria's Consort, Prince Albert, in 1852 for £31,500 and very little seems to have changed in the intervening years. Everyone who is invited, or commanded, to spend time at Balmoral is expected to join in the various sporting activities organised by Prince Philip. Excuses are not accepted; everyone, children included, obeys his rules. The daily programme, approved by Prince Philip, is printed and circulated to family, other guests and household staff the evening before, so no one has an excuse for not knowing what the next day will bring. The staff welcome the programme as it gives them notice of the number of outfits the day will require. Ladies have a particular interest in having advance notice when it comes to attire, as the different activities can mean they have to change up to four times a day: casual clothes for breakfast, followed by sporting outfits, then afternoon dresses for tea (an immovable feast in the everyday Royal calendar) and always long dresses at dinner. When Zara spends time at Balmoral – or Sandringham or Windsor – she is allocated a personal maid by the Queen, so unpacking and dressing becomes someone else's problem. She doesn't have a maid at home, saying she has no need of one, but when she is 'on duty' at Granny's, formality is the order of the day and a little help is most welcome.

Royal holidays are not restful affairs. Every day is planned from breakfast to bedtime, with every waking moment filled with walking, fishing and stalking in the hills. Even picnics are run on strictly military lines with extraordinary attention to detail. There is nothing casual about them. Sandwiches and bottles of beer are not just thrown into a hamper before the party sets off to find a suitable spot in the woods. When Prince Philip decides he wants a picnic, a 'recce' is first carried out by an advance party of senior footmen and security officers the day before. With the Balmoral estate criss-crossed by public footpaths, they have to make sure that no outsiders encroach upon the private tea party. Then on the day itself, liveried footmen leave early to set up the picnic site, making sure the barbecue is functioning correctly for the sausages and fillet steaks, and all the sandwiches have had their crusts cut off. Thermos flasks of hot tea and coffee are provided and the wine and beer is kept chilled in portable containers. The family draws the line at eating off and drinking from plastic plates and cups; everything they use is bone china and crystal. Prince Philip appoints himself as the head cook and he insists on lighting the barbecue, thereby convincing himself, if no one else, that he has done all the work. On one occasion he forgot to bring any matches and threw a tantrum, sending a footman a mile back to the castle to fetch some. The fact that it was his fault alone simply didn't enter his head.

Prince Charles was once asked what was his idea of a perfect holiday. He replied, 'Standing up to my thighs in icy water for hours on end in the River Dee, waiting for the salmon to bite.' Similarly, when Prince Philip was asked the same question, his answer was equally out-of-the-ordinary. His ideal vacation is to spend up to eight hours a day lying in damp gorse in the hills around Balmoral, stalking a stag.

If and when Zara and Mike get married, Mike is going to have to learn to enjoy country sports, and with this in mind, Zara has already bought him a shotgun that he uses to shoot rabbits on the Gatcombe estate. But he is nothing if not adaptable, and he already gets on well with both the Queen and Prince Philip, so there should be no great difficulties ahead.

When the young Zara and Peter joined their grandparents in Scotland in the summer months, they quickly learned to obey the rules, even if, at first, they took a little getting used to. One of their friends who was invited to spend a week at Balmoral said later it wasn't exactly a relaxing sort of place to stay. When she was a little girl, Zara loved to go into Ballater, the tiny town nearest to Balmoral, where just about every shop boasts a Royal-by-Appointment coat-of-arms over its door. In those days it was easy for her and Peter, with their cousins, William and Harry, to pop into the local sweet shops and spend their pocket money. There was little security and, as the people of the town were well used to seeing the Royal Family in their midst, no one bothered them. The locals were also very protective towards 'the Laird' and her family, keeping outsiders ignorant of their movements and never revealing what they bought in the shops. With security now changed out of all recognition, the idea of strolling into Ballater unaccompanied is a non-starter. Even the simplest shopping expedition becomes a major logistics exercise for the Royalty Protection Department. They carry out advance trips to survey the area and to make sure the premises their principals intend to visit are secure. Zara is still able to go about reasonably unchecked, but in order not to put too much pressure on the family and on their security officers, she tends to stay within the confines of the 50,000-acre Balmoral estate.

The Royals tend to 'go native' immediately they cross the border, donning tartan kilts and wearing the famous Balmoral tartan that is restricted to members of the Royal Family. Luncheons and dinners are formal affairs, with black tie being the order of the day for the men and the ladies all wearing evening gowns and tiaras. Dances are held in the Great Hall and from an early age the children were all taught the intricacies of Scottish Highland dancing. It's all a bit like Brigadoon, the fictional village immortalised in a Hollywood movie, where nothing had changed for over a hundred years. Even the late Prime Minister Harold Wilson described the place as a 'time warp'.

Another Royal favourite holiday destination is the ski slopes of Europe. For many years, Prince Charles and his sons have taken over a fashionable ski resort for a couple of weeks and the Princess Royal also used to enjoy the sport. Zara knows how to ski and she loves the idea of hurtling down a slope off-piste. She can never refuse a challenge, so when she was offered the chance of a ride down the famous Cresta Run, where tobogan speeds can reach up to 100 mph, she couldn't resist.

All the Royal Family loved the Royal Yacht and were very sad and disappointed when *Britannia* was decommissioned in 1997. When Zara and Peter were younger they were often taken on the Western Isles cruise around the coastline of Britain as the Queen and Prince Philip sailed up to Scotland for their annual summer break. The crew of *Britannia* got to know the children as they, together with William and Harry, played on deck, always under the watchful eye of one of the sailors, called 'Yotties', who was instructed to make sure they didn't fall overboard. On one occasion, when the then Lord Chamberlain, Lord Maclean, and his wife were on board, Zara was recruited to help Lady Maclean wind her knitting wool. Apparently, it kept her quiet for a couple of hours. And every year, *Britannia* was used as a headquarters by the Duke of Edinburgh during Cowes Week (a prestigious regatta held annually in August). The Royal Yacht would be anchored off the Isle of Wight, and Princess Anne would always come on board (she was taught to sail on Loch Muick by her father) and bring her children to see the races. They loved it and both Peter and Zara became competent sailors, having been taught the rudiments of handling a small sailing boat when they were in Scotland. The departure of *Britannia* was a great personal loss felt by all the Royal Family, including Peter and Zara.

In the summer of 2006, the Queen decided she would like to try and recreate a little of the happiness she enjoyed with *Britannia* and so she chartered a ship called the *Hebridian Princess* and invited 48 of her family and friends to join her on a cruise around the Western Isles. Zara was included but had to decline as the voyage came right in the middle of her training programme in the run-up to the World Championships in Aachen. Her Majesty fully understood Zara's situation and told her she should not interrupt her training under any circumstances. Zara was naturally disappointed, as she would have loved to be with Granny, but the result in Germany certainly made up for the loss of a wonderful holiday.

The Queen is a magnificent hostess who goes out of her way to ensure that all her guests, whether they are family who have been to Balmoral many times, or someone for whom this might be their first visit, enjoy themselves. She personally supervises the choice of rooms and visits them herself to see that everything is in perfect order before her guests arrive. There is only one aspect of Balmoral that perhaps some of her guests do not relish as much as she does, and that is the weather. The Queen never even notices the ever-present mist and creeping chill in the air. The rigours of a Highland summer mean that everyone wears woollen sweaters, even in August, and when one of Her Majesty's first-time guests was heard to remark about the lack of decent heating in the castle, she replied that he should 'wear an extra sweater'. All the Royal Family are the same; they simply do not concern themselves with comfort in the way that most people do. Log fires are burned throughout the summer at Balmoral because the Queen likes to see them blazing. They also now have central heating, but it is not entirely efficient in warming the one-hundred-and-fifty-year-old castle to modern standards. But, at least they now have a plentiful supply of hot water. Until a few years ago, there was a stampede in the mornings as everyone tried to get in first before the hot water ran out. Zara is a tough cookie and, even though she prefers the delights of a sun-drenched beach in the Bahamas, there is enough of the Windsor streak in her for her to enjoy Scotland in all winds and weathers.

At the moment, with Mike back in the England rugby XV, and Zara concentrating on her remaining equestrian ambitions, holidays are on the back burner. No doubt when the couple have achieved all they are aiming for, their thoughts will turn to a holiday, and – who knows – it could be a honeymoon.

16 AIMS AND AMBITIONS

'A lot of people have this perception that I don't actually do anything except lurch from one party to another. So it was nice to prove that I can do something reasonably well.' That was Zara Phillips, making the understatement of the year, having just won the European Three Day Event Championship at the age of 24 and proving that, indeed, there was something that she could do a lot more than just 'reasonably well'.

The difficulty that Zara has is that when one is known principally as the Queen's granddaughter and every story in the newspapers includes the words '. . . eleventh in line to the throne', everyone assumes, quite wrongly, that one only has to turn up at a horse trials event to win. But of course, you don't just turn up and become Champion of Europe overnight. It takes months of backbreaking hard work, determination and great deal of sheer talent.

To many riders, being top in Europe would be enough. But not Zara. She wants to be able to ride in, and win, every major championship in the world. You get the feeling that if she had her way, she would also like to be the next British woman to win the Wimbledon tennis singles. Her ambitions are unlimited.

When she won the European title she said she would hate it if she thought that would be the pinnacle of her riding career. There was so much more she knew she could achieve. She is even now schooling some of her younger horses in order to bring them up to the standard they will need to be in the running for the 2012 Olympic Games in London. She is not alone; all the leading riders in the world are doing the same; looking five or six years ahead. As Zara has put it, 'To win a medal at those games, in front of your home crowd, would be unbelievable.'

With ambitions like these, it is hard to believe that Zara never intended to make a career in eventing. 'To be honest, I wanted to be a physiotherapist, but I didn't get good enough grades,' she says. 'After that there wasn't anything else I was particularly good at, except for riding horses. I'm pretty relieved I've turned out OK at that.' OK is not the expression her parents and her British team-mates would use to describe Zara's riding. Fantastic, amazing, brilliant, and just about every other positive adjective you can find would be more appropriate.

The difficulty in having parents like Anne and Mark is that everyone expects Zara to try and do better than they have. When she started in eventing, she wanted to do the best she could, but she never had an overriding ambition to try and emulate her mother and father, and neither did she deliberately set out to do better than them. It was when she won her first major title, the European, that she admitted that she wanted to achieve more than her parents. Zara is extraordinarily proud of Anne and Mark and their success in eventing, but, as she says, it is impossible to make comparisons between what they did and what she has recently achieved. It's the same in almost every sport. It's a different era; standards have improved all round, and with every generation expectations increase. When she is pressed about her future ambitions, she will admit, albeit a little self-consciously, that she would like to do better than they did and achieve more.

What Zara finds difficult to understand is the British attitude to ambition. It has always been the way in Britain that it is all very well to succeed, as long as you give the impression that it doesn't matter and that you are not trying too hard. With Zara, winning does matter, and she doesn't care if people say she wants to win at all costs.

What is it that makes a winner? There are hundreds of very talented and skilful sportsmen and women around. They all practise for hours at a time and show skill that evades the ordinary man or woman in the street. But what is it about the McEnroes, the Borgs, the Navratilovas, the Piggotts, the Dettoris, the Beckhams, the New Zealand All Black rugby team, the Faldos of this world that changes them from being just extremely talented players into world-beaters? Pete Sampras won 14 Grand Slam titles; Jimmy Connors held the number one world ranking spot in tennis for 160 consecutive weeks. His mother told him that it was 'him against the world' and that he must win at all costs. It was mental attitude as much as physical skill and talent that made him a champion. It is aggression and animosity that earns respect from opponents. Elite athletes can afford to be gracious after the event, but never when it is taking place. It's an old adage in sport that 'nice guys' come second. Those I have spoken to at the top of their sport have all said the same thing: they want it more than anything else in the world. Nothing comes between them and their ultimate ambition. They all have the same look, the same hunger for victory. Success alone isn't enough; they have to win. When Mark Spitz won his seven gold Olympic swimming medals, who remembers who won the silver? When Mark Phillips won Badminton four times, who can recall the name of the runner-up? And it is not just the big occasions that count. Every event they take part in, from the smallest local meetings to the majors, whether it's golf, soccer, rugby, tennis or three day events, it's the same. They are just as hungry for victory no matter what the prize. It's a question of life and death to the true champions. If they lose any competition, a part of them dies. They suffer anguish and self-doubt, and question their own immortality – until the next time. Zara has a need to win, whether it's just a Gloucestershire point-to-point or the Badminton Horse Trials; the aim remains the same.

Everybody loves a winner. They look up to him or her and use words such as 'hero' and 'heroine' to describe them. They want to be near them and touch them, perhaps hoping that some of the magic will rub off on them. What they don't understand is that true champions are not like the rest of us. The Jack Nicklauses and Gary Players of this world are prepared to sacrifice anything, personal happiness and family included, in order to win. All champions have an extreme competitive drive; it's a characteristic common to them all. There is no compassion for their opponents; they are out to annihilate them. The difference between their drive and that of other people, who simply take part in competitions *hoping* to win, is that they are willing to destroy anyone who gets in their way and obliterate the opposition. There is a naked desire to defeat everyone else and emerge as number one in the world. It's a cut-throat approach that means the survival of the fittest. The rest go to the wall. Zara's older brother, Peter, who was a more-than-promising rugby player, and was chosen as a schoolboy international for Scotland, can attest to the fact that, to reach the very top in sport, talent and determination alone are not enough. You also have to be prepared to devote your life to the game (and in Peter's case, he also needed to grow a few more inches and put on several pounds to be truly competitive in rugby at an elite level). Still, Peter's mother was absolutely delighted when he won his first cap for Scotland, as she is Patron of the Scottish Rugby Union and never misses a game.

In eventing, physical courage is taken for granted. No one who didn't have it in spades would choose to sit on half a tonne of horseflesh travelling at 30 miles an hour and jumping fences that would withstand a full frontal attack by a tractor just for pleasure. So, while all the riders are brave, it is the ones who have the right mental attitude and the overall determination to succeed who end up winning the crown.

Zara is a driven woman who is one of the few British competitors who admits before a competition that she is there only to win. A favourite saying of hers is that she is going to give it her best shot and if anything else happens it won't be for lack of trying or lack of ambition. It's a refreshing attitude in these days when so many British sportsmen and women have got used to coming second. Only the young Scottish tennis wonder boy, Andy Murray, exudes Zara's level of confidence before he enters every match. He believes in himself, that he can beat all comers and, at the time of writing, his performance appears to be justifying that belief. Zara and Andy are two of a kind. What's more, she excels in the only sport in the world where men and women compete against one another. Women eventers use exactly the same cross-country course as the men, with the same time allowed and the same penalties incurred for faults. In no other sport are the sexes allowed to compete against each other on equal terms. In tennis women play only the best of three sets while men play the best of five – for the same money. So Zara's success must be judged against the standard set by not only the other female riders, but also against those of the world's leading male equestrians. When Zara sets targets for herself, they are not against the other women in her sport, but against everyone. She is ambitious to be the very best in the world, and that means better than all the rest, men and women. For her, the pursuit of excellence is the only road to the top and is nothing to be ashamed of.

One side effect of Zara's success has been an increase in the popularity of equestrianism among young girls in Britain. Apparently it has now replaced ballet lessons and tap dancing as a favourite pastime. In fact, the British Horse Society says riding has not been as popular since the early days of the last century, and they put much of the increased popularity down to Zara's achievements. In turn, this has meant a dramatic increase in house prices in rural areas, particularly in those parts of Gloucestershire around Gatcombe. The little girls just want to ride horses; their parents long to rub shoulders with the new World Champion – and her mother, if possible. Estate agents have been inundated with enquiries for properties that include a couple of acres where they can build a grass show-jumping ring and erect a few fences in one of the fields so the prospective owners' children can start what they hope will be a career like Zara's.

Throughout Britain house prices have begun to stabilise in recent years, but equestrian property specialists, who advertise in *Country Life* and *Horse and Hound*, are still enjoying a sales boom, with enquiries for country houses with stables and paddocks at an all-time high. Riding is no longer considered to be the elitist activity it once was, and with more people moving out of the cities into the country, property prices are rising accordingly. Houses near Gatcombe, which could be bought for £500,000 a couple of years ago, now change hands at prices nudging the £1 million mark, and they are being snapped up as soon as they come on the market.

Young couples working in high finance in the City have seen their annual bonuses go through the roof. Some now count them in the millions, and they are willing to spend if they can buy somewhere desirable, especially in the Royal county of Gloucestershire. And if little Ginny or Arabella can have Zara Phillips as a friend and neighbour, so much the better.

If Zara is aware of her influence on the property market, she isn't letting on, but as she knows a great many people in the area of Gatcombe, she must hear the talk about how prices have gone up. There's no indication that she and Mike Tindall are cashing in on the boom; perhaps if they had a couple of properties on the market and the buyers realised who was selling, they could make a small fortune.

Zara's ambitions lie in quite another direction. She has never claimed to be a businesswoman and she relies on expert advice to guide her in matters of finance. She is very interested in farming, having grown up in an agricultural environment. But with her, it's the hands-on, practical side – gathering the harvest and the day-to-day work of running a farm – that takes precedence over the business side. She has never had to worry about making a profit, and she never will. The plethora of rules and regulations that govern farming today do not concern her. She will always live in the country, and when she and Peter inherit Aston Farm – and presumably one of them will become the tenant of Gatcombe – it will be as gentlemen farmers and landowners, as Mark Phillips and the Princess Royal are at present.

Zara has her hands full concentrating on her stable of event horses. She believes there is plenty of scope to achieve even more than she already has. No one would deny that, having become World and European Champion at the age of 25, she could easily become the finest horsewoman the world has ever seen if she goes on in the same way. And if she is looking for a prime example of a 'mature' rider beating the world, then she could do no better than remember that Derek Allhusen won his Olympic gold medal for Great Britain at the ripe old age of 53.

It isn't only on the property market that Zara's success has had an effect. The growth in the popularity of riding has been such that a number of schools in England have introduced the sport into the curriculum. Public schools such as Millfield and Cheltenham Ladies College have always offered equestrianism, and one independent school near Bath has stabling for 60 horses and even offers riding scholarships, but now several state schools are finding there is a demand. It appears that boys and girls want to learn to ride and many of the schools are prepared to let them attend lessons at nearby stables if they do not have facilities of their own.

Schools that cater for children with special needs are finding that their children, some of whom come from very deprived homes and who may have been rather aggressive in the past, respond very well when they are taught to treat a horse with respect. It's not only riding but also looking after the animals that encourages the youngsters to attend school and improve their behaviour. In the past they may have been reluctant to turn up, but when they know they are going to have a riding lesson, they are enthusiastic. It is an unusual form of therapy, but if it works – and it looks as if it does – the staff are all for it.

Whether young people take up riding before they can walk, as Zara did, or learn a little later in life, it is another skill that can only benefit them. They won't all become world champion, of course, but there might be another Zara Phillips among them somewhere.

Major three day event trials are now held all over the world. In Kentucky in the United States, home of the famous Kentucky Derby, the trials are considered to be one of the highlights of the equestrian and social calendar. Another prestigious trials event is held in Adelaide, Australia, the country whose riders have been in the forefront of eventing at every World and Olympic Championships for many years. So for Zara, there are still plenty of mountains to conquer, plenty of events to win. To use a well-worn cliché, the world truly is her oyster.

Her immediate aim is a little nearer home. She wants to retain her European crown in Pratoni del Vivaro near Rome. Following the disappointment of having to withdraw from the Badminton Trials in May 2007 – which were also being used as an Olympic qualifier – in order to save Toytown from possible injury on the rock-hard ground, Zara is depending on the European Championships to qualify for the games. The Olympic title is the only one she has yet to win and all being well, she is determined to be in China in 2008.

17 WHAT NEXT?

B orn with extraordinary good fortune, blessed with outstanding talent and possessed of natural charisma, Zara
would seem to have the world at her feet. It would appear that
there is little she could want for and nothing she could not
achieve if she set her mind to it.

But having grown up trying desperately to rid herself of the
'Royal' tag, Zara has struggled to live a normal life. The
difficulty has been that, whatever the event – say her
non-Royal pals have invited her to a girl's night out or a
weekend get-together – she has always had to check her diary
months in advance to see that the dates don't clash with a
prince or princess's birthday, a Royal wedding anniversary or
one of the Queen's frequent special days. If they do, everything else has to take second place. There's no question of
Zara being able to turn down an invitation to Buckingham
Palace, Windsor Castle, Sandringham or Balmoral on the
grounds that she has a previous engagement. All her friends
now accept this and work their calendars around the Royal
year.

The fact that Zara cannot even call herself Lady Zara
Phillips (her brother would be a Viscount now if Mark had
accepted the earldom that was offered to him on his marriage

to Princess Anne) does not in any way make her less Royal than her titled cousins, William and Harry, Beatrice and Eugenie, and even little Louise, daughter of her Uncle Edward, the Earl of Wessex. She may be only 'Miss' Zara Phillips, but the similarity with any other 'Miss' in the country ends right there.

Zara does not trade on her Royal blood, but while she is far and away the most approachable member of the Royal Family, no one is left in the slightest doubt that any attempt at undue familiarity will be met with a distinctly Windsor chill. And, of course, it is not everyone who can pick up a telephone and be put through to the Queen no matter where she is. In Palace circles it is said that Her Majesty has given strict instructions that only three people are allowed to be connected to her at any time. One is her racing manager; the others are her grandson William – and Zara.

It would be nice to see some wholehearted praise in the mainstream press for Zara's achievements without the snide comments that usually accompany news of her latest success. It is not her fault that she was born with the proverbial silver spoon in her mouth. She would like nothing more than to be judged solely on her equestrian performance and for people to put aside the fact of her Royal connections. But that is never going to happen. If Zara were to win Olympic gold medals in Beijing and London back-to-back, it wouldn't make the slightest bit of difference. Someone will always claim it was because of the influence of Royalty.

The people who do influence Zara are, in order of importance, the Queen, the Princess Royal, the Duke of Edinburgh and Mark Phillips. Her stepfather, Tim Laurence, does not even enter the equation, and neither do her uncles, Charles, Andrew and Edward. She is fond of them all, in varying degrees, but she is not particularly concerned about their feelings for her. If she never saw any of them again, it would likely not give her too many sleepless nights. William and Harry are good mates, and she knows that one day she will be required to curtsey to William – if she can control her giggles – but his influence over her does not match that of her parents and grandparents.

The Queen's influence is not merely in relation to Zara's riding; she has also guided her throughout her life in taste and manners. Zara shares her grandmother's interests, which are those of a typical countrywoman of her class. They both love horses and dogs and believe in upholding the life of the community. Neither is academic, but both are highly intelligent. The Queen and Zara have a dislike for authority. When driving, neither likes wearing a seat belt, but only the Queen can get away with it, and she only drives on private roads. When 'on duty' in public, both are ultra-conventional; in private they both like to flout conformity. The Queen cannot be seen to support hunting now that it has been outlawed, but secretly she is known to have been dismayed when this most commonplace of all country sports became illegal. Zara too would still be riding to hounds every week in the season, if it were not that by doing so she would be drawing unwelcome attention to those who still insist on their right to hunt.

The Queen and Zara share a delightful sense of humour. The more ridiculous the story, the better. When Zara had her tongue pierced in a tattoo parlour, her grandmother thought it was hilarious, but she kept her opinion to herself. There was no word of disapproval; the Queen Mother thought the stud was the result of some sort of initiation rite that Zara had undergone at Gordonstoun, much to the secret amusement of the rest of the family, and nobody enlightened her.

Zara is a well-balanced, rounded and remarkably normal person and even though she is still only in her mid-twenties, if there is a single quality that can be attributed to Zara Phillips it is determination. She is single-minded to a frightening degree, and that propels her towards winning at all costs. She is determined to succeed at anything she attempts. When she played hockey at Cheltenham Ladies College – though she was never a student there – it was with an aggressive attitude that made her a fearsome opponent. According to some of the girls who played on the same team, they were very glad they weren't facing her, as she looked for the ball constantly and tackled with a ferociousness rarely seen in well brought up young ladies. One of her contemporaries commented that she has boundless energy and is never happy unless she is doing something that is physically exhausting, hence the bungee jumping, surfing, swimming and, of course, her pursuit of the toughest of all equestrian disciplines.

Zara has been called her mother's daughter because of her non-nonsense attitude and her willingness to tackle anything that's put in front of her. But she is also her father's child, with her resolute belief in herself and a stubborn refusal to accept defeat. Because Mark Phillips spent years in his former wife's shadow, as she was the one with the high public profile, performing Royal duties with an assurance that comes only from an in-built sense of superiority common to every member of the Royal Family, many people mistakenly thought he was a little too diffident. What they did not realise is that what they regard as shyness on his part is simply the fact that if he hasn't got anything to say, he prefers to keep silent. But Mark is his own man. He knows exactly what he wants to do and no one will force him to do otherwise. His physical courage has never been in doubt. As a cavalry officer (1st The Queen's Dragoon Guards), he was extremely popular with his men and with his fellow officers, one of whom, Eric Grounds, was best man at his wedding in Westminster Abbey.

Zara has inherited many of the characteristics of her parents. Her love of sport is self-evident, but she also is a compassionate young woman, who realises how privileged she is and understands the problems many of her less fortunate contemporaries face. Having a broad education and also having travelled extensively without the cushion of Royal protection, she has experienced more of the ordinary world than her mother, who, of course, has travelled many thousands of miles on public duties, but always with every detail planned by others well in advance. The Princess Royal enjoys travel, but who wouldn't when the Royal Train, Royal Flight and Royal Yacht have been at your disposal for most of your life? The Princess always has the final say in all her journeys, but she has never bought a rail or airline ticket in her life, and she never will. It's a Palace mantra that whenever a Royal flies, an invisible purple carpet unrolls above, below and on either side of their aircraft so that nothing can interfere with the Royal progress. An air traffic controller of my acquaintance explained that there is nothing magic about it; it is just that all other flights are warned not to come within several miles of any aircraft carrying Royalty.

Zara is not yet in that category, but doors have opened to her that would have remained firmly closed if she had not been who she is. Despite this, she has seen something of life that has been denied even to the Princess Royal, and certainly almost every other member of the Royal Family. During her gap year, Zara travelled alone in Australia and New Zealand, unlike William and Harry, who also journeyed abroad but under the watchful eyes of their ever-present protection officers and with every step of the way arranged months in advance by Clarence House – and approved by the Queen.

Zara chose to make her life's work in a sport where position, rank and money count for little. Well, perhaps money helps. But competitive three day events are ferocious competitions and no one was ever going to give way to Zara because of her Royal relations. She says if only those watching and criticising could see her at six o'clock on a freezing cold morning, mucking out the stables at Gatcombe, then riding four or five horses all day, and finally making sure they are all tucked up at night, they might not be so fast to condemn.

In her dealings with the charities with which she is involved, Zara demonstrates a practical knowledge of their problems and an in-depth understanding of their work, so that she has become much more than just another celebrity figurehead. She is fully aware of the value of her name; it has been proven many times at the functions she has attended, and the organisers of her charities say her presence at a gala dinner or reception can add thousands to the sums they hope to raise.

Because she was born with so many advantages, Zara felt from an early age the need to prove her worth. She knows that whatever she attempts, there will always be someone who will claim it is only through being the daughter of the Princess Royal and the granddaughter of the Queen that she will succeed. It may irritate her, but she knows how hard she works and she tries to put such carping out of her mind.

Zara's private life has been something of an open book in the past, and she has only herself to blame for that. Now that she has settled down with Mike, things have quietened down considerably and while, at the time of writing, the couple haven't yet announced an engagement, it is probably not far off. They are expected to marry sometime in 2008, once the Olympic Games in China are ended. Tindall has been a calming influence on Zara and while their domestic living arrangements may be slightly unconventional for a member of the Royal Family, few people see anything unusual these days in modern young couples living together. We are not likely to see Prince William moving in with a girlfriend, but then he is eventual heir to the throne and the Queen – and the Archbishop of Canterbury – would likely frown on such an arrangement. In Zara's case, she is so far down the line of succession that her personal love life is not regarded as endangering the monarchy in the slightest. Even when she lived with Richard Johnson, with the ensuing publicity that followed the feature they sold to *Hello!* magazine, no one at Buckingham Palace thought it worth making a fuss. The Princess Royal and Mark Phillips didn't object, so why should anyone else?

Of course, when Princess Anne married Mark, it was the first time in nine hundred years that a British Royal princess had been allowed to marry the man she wanted without any thought of political or monarchical expediency, so Zara could hardly be expected to marry a European Royal, or even a British aristocrat, purely to please the Queen. Not that Her Majesty would ever try to influence her granddaughter in her choice of husband; she is far too realistic, and she knows that even William and Harry, who are far more important in the Royal scheme of things, will choose their own partners when the time comes – subject to discreet Royal approval (although realistically, we are hardly likely to see a young woman from a local comprehensive school trotting up the aisle at Westminster Abbey on William's arm – freedom goes only so far in a constitutional monarchy and democracy just doesn't come into it).

Zara is going to have to continue to make her own way in life, but will never confront the sort of financial problems that other young people face. Her trust fund will mature and see her safely into middle age; when her mother dies, she and Peter will inherit substantial sums and, as previously stated, on her father's death, she and Peter will divide the entire Gatcombe estate, including Aston Farm, itself worth over £2 million, between them. At the present time the estate is valued at £7 million. What it will be worth in years to come is anybody's guess.

Zara is not involved in Royal duties at the moment, but with the Queen now 81 and the Duke of Edinburgh 86, the Prince of Wales not far off 60, the Princess Royal in her late fifties, and the Gloucesters and Kents approaching or, in some cases, past retiring age, there is shortly going to be a need for a younger, personable member of the family to take on some duties and help relieve the burden on the older Royals. Prince William and Prince Harry still have some years' service to complete in the armed forces before they are able to take on full-time responsibilities in 'The Firm', while Peter Phillips already has a job in motor racing and does not have the personality, or wish, to become a public figure. Zara has everything to offer, except a title, and the public would welcome seeing her perform as a stand-in for her mother occasionally.

She would need some tuition and, after her acceptance speech at the BBC Sports Personality of the Year ceremony, it would seem coaching in public speaking would also be in order. But the Princess Royal could easily take on that task, and Zara already looks good and has a natural grace that will stand her in good stead. She had inherited an excellent sense of duty and, once she has achieved all she wants in the equestrian world, she will be a fantastic asset to the Royal Family. She may find the restrictions of life as a full-time Royal frustrating, but in order to relieve the pressure on the older family members, I believe Zara would willingly accept an active role, at least until her cousins, William and Harry, are able to take on their Royal responsibilities. Until now she has not had to endure the never-ending attention of the Royalty and Diplomatic Protection Department. Her mother grew up accepting the presence of armed police officers as normal, but Zara, when she is alone, or with friends, does not warrant such surveillance. If she does take on public duties, she will have to get used to having someone with her at all times and that may be one of the less pleasant aspects of her future life. She has seen how restricted her mother's life has been because of the need for the constant presence of the duty policemen, and Zara hates the idea of being cramped in this way.

Zara's has been the most remarkable of equestrian careers, reaching the pinnacle of the sport within less than three years of becoming a full-time participant, and she is still well below the age at which three day event riders are expected to be at their peak. It is no secret that Zara has ambitions to ride in next year's Olympic Games in China, and as long as Toytown stays fit and injury-free, she will almost certainly be in the reckoning for inclusion in the British team. Can she complete the trio of equestrian triumphs by adding an Olympic medal to her European and World titles? The people who know about these things say there is no reason why she cannot achieve her ambition. She has already beaten both her parents' World Championship ratings, but victory at Badminton, which her father won four times, has so far eluded her.

Interest in equestrian sports is at an all-time high following Zara's success at the World Championships. There's been a huge surge in popularity, with over a million horses now registered in Britain and two million riding every month. Many people still believe that riding is an expensive and elitist pastime, and it is true that money can flow in only one direction when you own a horse. But then, a reasonable mount can be bought today for around £3,000, less than half the cost of the cheapest new car. Obviously there are extras like saddlery, riding gear, stabling and vets' bills to take into account, but nevertheless, the old image of riding being restricted to spoiled upper-class girls is fast disappearing. The Olympic Games, which will be seen by millions on television around the world, will raise the profile of riding even more and if Zara, or any of the British team, wins a medal, its popularity will soar.

As an intelligent young woman with an enquiring mind, Zara likes to take her own decisions, which, so far, she has been allowed to do. She has an unshakeable belief in the monarchy while at the same time possessing a tendency to speak her mind. Apart from her ill-conceived interview with *Hello!*, she has never placed the Royal Family in an embarrassing situation, and that one experience is not likely to be repeated. Her position within the family, albeit far-removed from the throne itself, guarantees she has a glamorous appeal. Combined with her sporting achievements, good looks and casual charm, she has proved irresistible to sponsors and public alike.

Once she has fulfilled her riding ambitions (and she will still only be 31 when the London Olympic Games are held in 2012), she may play an increasingly prominent role in the life of the Royal Family. She has the charisma and personality to engage the affection and attention of people who are perhaps looking for a new kind of Royal figure: one who captures the public's imagination. One of her greatest qualities is her ability to get on with people from all walks of life and of all ages and classes. It is a formidable accomplishment that seems to have come quite naturally to Zara.

She is talented and down to earth, with a combination of strength and vulnerability in her character. She loves life and because of her success on the sporting field at such an early age, the public, young people particularly, feel they can identify with her. They also like the fact that she is opinionated and not afraid to voice those opinions, in other words, a formidable young woman who will be an invaluable asset to the Royal Family in the years to come.

APPENDIX I

ZARA PHILLIPS' MAJOR EQUESTRIAN RESULTS

Year	Venue	Horse	Position
2001	Windsor	Toytown	Completed CCI
2001	Burgie CCI	Toytown	13th
2002	Wiendorf	Toytown	Silver Medal European Young Rider
2003	Chatsworth CCI	Toytown	10th
2003	Luhmuhlen CCI	Toytown	5th
2003	Gatcombe Park	Toytown	4th
2003	Burghley	Toytown	2nd
2004	Luhmuhlen	Springleaze Macaroo	7th
2004	Martinvast	Springleaze Macaroo	9th
2005	Nallindenisk	Red Baron	6th
2005	Ballindenisk	Tsunami 11	4th
2005	Lumuhlen	Toytown	2nd
2005	Gatcombe Park	Red Baron	3rd
2005	Blenheim (European Championships)	Toytown	1st (Gold, individual and team)

2005	Necame	Ardfield Magic Star	8th
2006	Kreuth	Ardfield Magic Star	12th
2006	Burnham Market	Toytown	15th
2006	Bramham	Ardfield Magic Star	10th
2006	Aachen (World Championships)	Toytown	1st (Gold medal & World Champion)

APPENDIX II

WORLD EQUESTRIAN CHAMPIONSHIP 2006 – EVENTING TEAM RESULTS

Place	Rider	Horse	Score
1	**Germany**		**156.00**
	Frank OSTHOLT	Air Jordan 2	50.90
	Hinrich ROMEIKE	Marius	52.40
	Bettina HOY	Ringwood Cockatoo	52.70
	Ingrid KLIMKE	Sleep Late	96.70
2	**Great Britain**		**180.00**
	Zara PHILLIPS	Toytown	46.70
	Daisy DICK	Spring Along	64.30
	William FOX-PITT	Tamarillo	69.00
	Mary KING	Call Again Cavalier	81.10
3	**Australia**		**197.30**
	Clayton FREDERICKS	Ben Alone Time	48.80
	Megan JONES	Kirby Park Irish	70.10
	Andrew HOY	Master Monarch	78.40
	Sonja JOHNSON	Ringwould Jaguar	1000.00

4	United States of America		198.10
	Amy TRYON	Poggio II	50.70
	Kimberly SEVERSON	Winsome Adante	71.70
	Will FAUDREE	Antigua	75.70
	Heidi WHITE	Northern Spy	89.20

5	Sweden		218.20
	Magnus GÄLLERDAL	Keymaster	53.80
	Dag ALBERT	Who's Blitz	67.50
	Linda ALGOTSSON	My Fair Lady	96.90
	Viktoria CALERBÄCK	Ballys Geronimo	129.60

6	New Zealand		221.70
	Hellan TOMPKINS	Glengarrick	53.80
	Andrew NICHOLSON	Lord Killinghurst	79.60
	Caroline POWELL	Lenamore	88.30
	Joe MEYER	Snip 2	170.80

7	France		312.90
	Gilles VIRICEL	Blakring	77.70
	Nicolas TOUZAINT	Hidalgo de l'Ile	91.00
	Jean TEULERE	Espoir de la Mare	144.20
	Arnaud BOITEAU	Expo du Moulin	1000.00

8	Netherlands		358.00
	Jan van BEEK	La Cru	95.00
	Chantal MEGCHELENBRINK	Jacker Cracker	127.20
	Werner GEVEN	Esker Riada	135.80

9	Ireland		361.80
	Niall GRIFFIN	Lorgaine	98.80
	Sarah WARDELL	Kincluny	103.90
	Michael RYAN	Old Road	159.10
	Geoff CURRAN	Balladeer Alfred	185.00

10	Austria		1190.00
	Harald AMBROS	Miss Ferrari	92.70
	Harald SIEGL	Nebelwerfer	97.30
	Harald RIEDL	Davigna	1000.00

11	Italy		1227.20
	Fabio MAGNI	Loro Piana Southern	96.50
	Susanna BORDONE	Carrera	130.70
	Matco BIASIA	Ecu	1000.00
	Alice BERTOLI	Oakengrove Milan	1000.00

12	Belgium		1242.30
	Karin DONCKERS	Gazelle De La	64.40
	Carl BOUCKAERT	Rampant Lion	177.90
	Sandra ODELBERG	Rainman	1000.00

13	Poland		1369.40
	Pawel SPISAK	Weriusz	145.80
	Lukasz KAZMIERCZAK	Ostler	223.60
	Pawel RUTKOWSKI	Fordanser	1000.00

14	Denmark		2082.60
	Peter T. FLARUP	Silver Ray	82.60
	May-Britt KATTRUP	Victor	1000.00
	Morten HAUGAARD	My Hamlet	1000.00

APPENDIX III

WORLD EQUESTRIAN CHAMPIONSHIP 2006 – EVENTING INDIVIDUAL RESULTS

Place	Rider	NF	Horse	Dressage		Cross		Jumping		Total	*
				Score	%	Obstacle	Time	Obstacle	Time		
1	Zara PHILLIPS	GBR	Toytown	41.70	72.20			4	1	46.70	yes
2	Clayton FREDERICKS	AUS	Ben Along Time	44.40	70.40		4.4			48.80	yes
3	Amy TRYON	USA	Poggio II	50.70	66.20					50.70	yes
4	Frank OSTHOLT	GER	Air Jordan 2	46.90	68.73			4		50.90	yes
5	Hinrich ROMEIKE	GER	Marius	52.40	65.07					52.40	yes
6	Bettina HOY	GER	Ringwood Cockatoo	36.50	75.67		7.2	8	1	52.70	yes
7	Heelan TOMPKINS	NZL	Glengarrick	49.80	66.80			4		53.80	yes
8	Magnus GÄLLERDAL	SWE	Keymaster	47.40	68.40		2.4	4		53.80	yes
9	Sharon HUNT	GBR	Tankers Town	47.40	68.40		13.2		1	61.60	yes
10	Karim Florent LAGHOUAG	FRA	Make My Day	63.70	57.53					63.70	yes
11	Oliver TOWNEND	GBR	Flint Curtis	62.00	58.67				2	64.00	yes

Place	Rider	NF	Horse	Dressage		Cross		Jumping		Total	*
				Score	%	Obstacle	Time	Obstacle	Time		
12	Daisy DICK	GBR	Spring Along	64.30	57.13					64.30	yes
13	Karin DONCKERS	BEL	Gazelle De La	45.20	69.87		13.2	4	2	64.40	yes
14	Dag ALBERT	SWE	Who's Blitz	61.50	59.00			4	2	67.50	yes
15	William FOX-PITT	GBR	Tamarillo	45.00	70.00	20	4			69.00	yes
16	Megan JONES	AUS	Kirby Park Irish	44.10	70.60	20	6			70.10	yes
17	Kimberly SEVERSON	USA	Winsome Adante	40.90	72.73	20	6.8	4		71.70	yes
18	Yoshiaki OIWA	JPN	Fifth Avenue Fame	74.50	50.33					74.50	yes
19	Will FAUDREE	USA	Antigua	63.30	57.80		8.4	4		75.70	yes
20	Gilles VIRICEL	FRA	Blakring	61.70	58.87		16			77.70	yes
21	Andreas DIBOWSKI	GER	Serve Well	40.90	72.73	20	13.2	4		78.10	yes
22	Andrew HOY	AUS	Master Monarch	47.60	68.27	20	6.8	4		78.40	yes
23	Andrew NICHOLSON	NZL	Lord Killinghurst	49.60	66.93	20		4	6	79.60	yes
24	Mary KING	GBR	Call Again Cavalier	51.90	65.40	20	9.2			81.10	yes
25	Peter T. FLARUP	DEN	Silver Ray	74.60	50.27			8		82.60	yes
26	Caroline POWELL	NZL	Lenamore	66.30	55.80	20	2			88.30	yes
27	Heidi WHITE	USA	Northern Spy	50.40	66.40		30.8	8		89.20	yes
28	Nicolas TOUZAINT	FRA	Hildago de l'Ile	47.00	68.67	20	20	4		91.00	yes
29	Jean Renaud ADDE	FRA	Haston D'Elpegère	61.70	58.87		18.4	8	3	91.10	yes

30	Phillip DUTTON	AUS	Connaught	51.70	65.53	20	12.4	8		92.10	yes
31	Harald AMBROS	AUT	Miss Ferrari	58.30	61.13	20	14.4	12		92.70	yes
32	Jan VAN BEEK	NED	La Cru	58.20	61.20		22.8		2	95.00	yes
33	Fabio MAGNI	ITA	Loro Piana Southern	58.50	61.00		38			96.50	no
34	Ingrid KLIMKE	GER	Sleep Late	39.10	73.93	40	17.6			96.70	no
35	Linda ALGOTSSON	SWE	My Fair Lady	48.90	67.40	20	18	8	2	96.90	yes
36	Harald SIEGL	AUT	Nebelwerfer	60.90	59.40		26.4	8	2	97.30	yes
37	Niall GRIFFIN	IRL	Lorgaine	57.40	61.73		18.4	20	3	98.80	no
38	Sarah WARDELL	IRL	Kincluny	58.50	61.00	20	16.4	8	1	103.90	yes
39	Tobias GRÖNBERG	SWE	Amaretto	66.50	55.67	20	31.2	8		125.70	yes
40	Carlos Eduardo PARO	BRA	Political Mandate	72.80	51.47	20	25.2	4	5	127.00	yes
41	Chantal MEGCHELENBRINK	NED	Jacker Cracker	67.20	55.20		50	4	6	127.20	no
42	Karen O'CONNOR	USA	Upstage	59.80	60.13	40	20	8		127.80	no
43	Viktoria CARLERBÄCK	SWE	Bally's Geronimo	54.80	63.47	40	30.8		4	129.60	no
44	Susanna BORDONE	ITA	Carrera	48.90	67.40	20	48.8	8	5	130.70	no
45	Jan THOMPSON	USA	Task Force	53.30	64.47	40	27.2	12		132.50	no
46	Werner GEVEN	NED	Esker Riada	69.80	53.47	20	34	12		135.80	yes
47	Jean TEULERE	FRA	Espoir de la Mare	54.60	63.60	40	29.6	8	12	144.20	no
48	Pawel SPISAK	POL	Weriusz	58.20	61.20	60	19.6	8		145.80	no
49	Samantha ALBERT	JAM	Before I Do It	59.80	60.13	40	57.6		1	158.40	no

Place	Rider	NF	Horse	Dressage		Cross		Jumping		Total	*
				Score	%	Obstacle	Time	Obstacle	Time		
50	Michael RYAN	IRL	Old Road	63.30	57.80	60	22.8	12	1	159.10	no
51	Joe MEYER	NZL	Snip	50.40	66.40	85	18.4	12	5	170.80	no
52	Carl BOUCKAERT	BEL	Rampant Lion	63.30	57.80	60	49.6		5	177.90	no
53	Geoff CURRAN	IRL	Balladeer Alfred	68.00	54.67	60	40	12	5	185.00	no
54	Lukasz KAZMIERCZAK	POL	Ostler	55.40	63.07	105	41.2	16	6	223.60	no
55	Viachaslau POITA	BLR	Energiya	67.80	54.80	60	93.6	28		249.40	no
56	Carlos GRAVE	POR	Laughton Hills	71.30	52.47	125	101.2	12		309.50	no
—	Marco BIASIA	ITA	ECU	EL 3rd Horse Insp.							no
—	Dirk SCHRADE	GER	Sindy 43	WD before 3rd Horse Insp.							no
—	Luisa PALLI	ITA	Axia II	WD before 3rd Horse Insp.							no
—	Donna SMITH	NZL	Call Me Clifton	RT XC							no
—	Pila PANTSU	FIN	Ypäjä Karuso	RT XC							no
—	Shane ROSE	AUS	All Luck	RT XC							no
—	Eddy STIBBE	AHO	Dusky Moon	RT XC							no
—	Sonja JOHNSON	AUS	Ringwould Jaguar	RT XC							no

*Qualifying result (No=Rider and horse not registered; QR=Horse not registered; QH=Rider not registered). NF=Nationality.

ACKNOWLEDGEMENTS

There are many people who should be thanked for their kindness and help with this book, but as most of them spoke to me on the strict understanding that I would not reveal their identities, I will respect their privacy and confidentiality.

Those who made no such request however include: Richard Meade, David Pogson, Margaret Holder, Jayne Fincher, Jessica Skinner, Brian Goode, Ingrid Seward, Joe Little, Maureen Rose, David Emanuel, Vicki Woods and research staff at the National Library of Wales, Aberystwyth. At Virgin Books, Davina Russell edited the text with infinite patience and great skill, Sarah Flint chose the photographs, while Ed Faulkner is the man who originally proposed the idea of the book about Zara, for which many thanks. I am also very grateful to my agent, Gordon Wise at Curtis Brown, for his enthusiasm and unflagging energy on my behalf.

As usual, all opinions, unless from quoted sources, are mine and mine alone – *mea culpa*.

SELECT BIBLIOGRAPHY

Among the books consulted were:

Allison, R & Riddell, S, *The Royal Encyclopedia*, Macmillan (1991)

Bradford, Sarah, *Elizabeth: A Biography of HM The Queen*, Heinemann (1996)

Clinton, Bill, *My Life*, Hutchinson (2004)

Dimbleby, Jonathan, *The Prince of Wales*, Little, Brown (1994)

Flamini, Roland, *Sovereign*, Delocorte Press (1991)

Hoey, Brian, *Her Majesty*, HarperCollins (2002)

Hoey, Brian, *Mountbatten*, Sidgewick & Jackson (1994)

Hoey, Brian, *Princess Anne*, Country Life Books (1984)

Johnson, Richard, *Out of the Shadows*, Greenwater (2002)

Judd, Dennis, *Prince Phillip*, Michael Joseph (1980)

Lacey, Robert, *Majesty*, Hutchinson (1977)

Longford, Elizabeth, *Elizabeth R*, Weidenfeld & Nicholson (1983)

Pimlott, Ben, *The Queen*, HarperCollins (1996)

Seward, Ingrid, *Royal Children*, HarperCollins (1993)

Warwick, Christopher, *Princess Margaret*, Weidenfeld & Nicholson (1983)

INDEX